Pleasure and Change

The Berkeley Tanner Lectures

The Tanner Lectures on Human Values, which honour the American scholar, industrialist, and philanthropist Obert Clark Tanner, are presented annually at each of nine universities in the United States and England. They were established at the University of California, Berkeley, beginning in the 2000/1 academic year. This volume is the second in a series of books based on the Berkeley Tanner Lectures. In this volume we include the lectures that Frank Kermode presented in November 2001, along with the responses of the three invited commentators on that occasion—Geoffrey Hartman, John Guillory, and Carey Perloff—and a final rejoinder by Professor Kermode. The volume is edited by Robert Alter, who also contributes an Introduction. We have established the Berkeley Tanner Lectures Series in the belief that these distinguished lectures, together with the lively debates stimulated by their presentation in Berkeley, deserve to be made available to a wider audience. Additional volumes are now in preparation.

ROBERT POST
SAMUEL SCHEFFLER
Series Editors

Volumes Published in the Series
Joseph Raz, *The Practice of Value*
Edited by R. Jay Wallace
With Christine M. Korsgaard, Roberet Pippin, and Bernard Williams

Pleasure and Change
The Aesthetics of Canon

FRANK KERMODE

With Commentaries by
GEOFFREY HARTMAN
JOHN GUILLORY
CAREY PERLOFF

Edited and Introduced by
ROBERT ALTER

OXFORD
UNIVERSITY PRESS

2004

OXFORD
UNIVERSITY PRESS

Oxford   New York

Auckland   Bangkok   Buenos Aires   Cape Town   Chennai
Dar es Salaam   Delhi   Hong Kong   Istanbul   Karachi   Kolkata
Kuala Lumpur   Madrid   Melbourne   Mexico City   Mumbai   Nairobi
São Paulo   Shanghai   Singapore   Taipei   Tokyo   Toronto

''Pleasure and Change: The Aesthetics of Canon'' by Frank Kermode was delivered as a
Tanner Lecture on Human Values at the University of California, Berkeley, 2001.
Printed with permission of the Tanner Lectures on Human Values, a corporation,
University of Utah, Salt Lake City, Utah, USA.

Published by Oxford University Press, Inc.
198 Madison Avenue, New York, New York 10016

www.oup.com

Oxford is a registered trademark of Oxford University Press

Library of Congress Cataloging-in-Publication Data
Kermode, Frank, 1919–
Pleasure and change: the aesthetics of canon / Frank Kermode
with commentaries by Geoffrey Hartman, John Guillory,
Carey Perloff; edited and introduced by Robert Alter.
p. cm. — (The Berkeley Tanner lectures)
Includes index.
ISBN 0-19-517137-3
1. Canon (Literature) 2. Literature—Psychological aspects.
I. Alter, Robert. II. Title. III. Series.
PN81.K425 2004
809—dc22   2003060974

1 3 5 7 9 8 6 4 2

Printed in the United States of America
on acid-free paper

Contents

REPLY TO COMMENTATORS

List of Contributors

SIR FRANK KERMODE is Professor Emeritus of English at the University of Cambridge. One of the preeminent critics in the English-speaking world, he has written on a broad range of topics from the New Testament to Shakespeare, the Romantics, Wallace Stevens, and literary theory. Among his many books, three that are especially relevant to the issue of canon formation are *The Classic*, *Forms of Attention*, and *History and Value*.

ROBERT ALTER is Professor of Hebrew and Comparative Literature at the University of California at Berkeley. His work has been concerned with the European and American novel, with literary aspects of the Hebrew Bible, and with literary history and theory. Two of his books pertinent to the subject of this volume are *The Pleasures of Reading in an Ideological Age* and *Canon and Creativity*.

JOHN GUILLORY is Professor of English and Chair of the Department of English at New York University. He is the author of three volumes of criticism, *What's Left of Theory?*, *Poetic Authority*, and *Cultural Capital: The Problem of Literary Canon Formation*. The last of these has exerted considerable influence on current discussions of the canon.

GEOFFREY HARTMAN, Professor Emeritus of English and Comparative Literature at Yale University, is the author of some two dozen books and has been one of the leading interpreters of English Romantic poetry. His early study of Wordsworth, Hopkins, Rilke, and Valéry, *The Unmediated Vision*, is a seminal work, and he has devoted a series of important volumes to the state of literary criticism, French poststructuralist thought, remembering the Holocaust, and related topics.

CAREY PERLOFF is Artistic Director of the American Conservatory Theater in San Francisco, one of the country's leading repertory companies. Under her directorship A.C.T. has mounted a wide variety of critically acclaimed productions, from the Greek tragedians to Shakespeare to Tom Stoppard and younger contemporaries.

Pleasure and Change

Introduction

ROBERT ALTER

The pages that follow are a record of Sir Frank Kermode's Tanner Lectures, presented at the University of California at Berkeley in November 2001, and of the lively exchange around them generated by three respondents.

The issue of the canon, and what may be suspect or even insidious about the canon, has been repeatedly debated in academic circles since the early 1990s. This debate has been for the most part dictated by the widespread politicization of literary studies variously alluded to by Frank Kermode, Geoffrey Hartman, and John Guillory. If canon formation is motivated, as academic critics have frequently claimed, by some sort of "collusion with the discourses of power," in Kermode's summary of this view, the canon itself must be viewed with a cold eye of suspicion as a potential vehicle of coercion, exclusion, and covertly ideological manipulation. Kermode clearly rejects such notions, and, indeed, none of the discussants seems inclined to defend them, with the marginal exception of a rather vague gesture toward the political at the end of Hartman's essay. One of the virtues, in fact, of Kermode's proposals for thinking about what makes literary works canonical is that instead of polemically engaging the ideological definition of the canon (a dispute that has been conducted all too frequently), he simply bypasses it, perhaps as unworthy of debate, and instead lays out a different set of terms. Two of his three central terms—*pleasure* and *change*—appear as the titles of his two lectures, and the third is *chance*.

This last term, I would note, is barely addressed in the three responses, perhaps because of its seeming oddness but more probably because it does not readily lend itself to general explanatory theories. It might well deserve to be given more weight than the discussion here registers. Because we all like to have firm handles to grasp when we try to make sense of complex phenomena, the usual assumptions we make about the canon are that it is somehow intentional, possibly on the part of writers who aspire to enter it and clearly on the part of communities of readers who fix the canon, and that, in keeping with this intentionality, it reflects certain intrinsic qualities in the works included, whether formal, aesthetic, moral, social, psychological, or ideological. Kermode, citing a couple of examples, suggests that canon formation might be more like a chess game in which from time to time the pieces get scrambled by some blind force of circumstance.

There are, for example, 150 psalms in the canonical biblical collection, which would appear to be a kind of anthology spanning several centuries of poetic production. Some of these, of course, are magnificent poems. At least a few others are rather formulaic and may strike many modern readers as relatively undistinguished. Did these poems make it into what would become the biblical canon because the ancient editors deemed them the 150 finest instances of psalmodic poetry in Hebrew, or because they best expressed the pieties of Israelite monotheism? Some of the psalms were obviously preserved because they had become fixtures in the temple service. But chance cannot be entirely excluded from the making of the canonical anthology. One is haunted by the thought of a Hebrew psalm as sublime as Psalm 8 or as eloquently moving as Psalm 23 that did not survive as part of the canon for the simple reason that the scroll on which it was recorded turned to dry dust in an ancient urn before the editors could include it in their authoritative collection. Kermode's notion of chance is surely worth keeping in mind as a salutary admonition to bland confidence in whatever generalizations about the canon we may make.

Of the two other concepts put forth in the lectures, the notion of change does not elicit any real debate in the responses. It seems unexceptionable that as cultural eras change and as we change individually, or even idiosyncratically, the canon we imagine we are reading changes as well, in regard to both how we see the works and what works are included. It should be noted that change in the canon is by no means associated with the old dispensation of literary criticism to which Kermode refers somewhat elegiacally at the beginning of his first lecture (and in my view, both Hartman and Guillory imagine too substantive a connection between that elegiac prelude and the propositions about the canon that follow). On the contrary, the critics of the old dispensation tended to assume a degree of timelessness about the canon that has come to be rejected by almost all contemporary observers, including Kermode. Matthew Arnold conceived his touchstones, drawn from such texts as the *Iliad*, the *Divine Comedy*, and the plays of Shakespeare, as enduringly valid, not really subject to change. The revisionist critics of Kermode's youth, such as F. R. Leavis, with his notorious list of only four great English novelists (two of them women), or, in America, Cleanth Brooks, with his polemic marginalization of the Romantic poets, were composing new canonical lists not in open concession to inevitable change but rather on the assumption that their misguided predecessors had got it wrong and that the canon they were now proclaiming would henceforth be recognized as the valid one. Change, as Kermode delineates it, is a mark of the provisionality of canons, which was not an idea much in favor under the old dispensation. In precisely this regard, I think Guillory is mistaken in contending that Kermode advocates a "return to the notion of touchstone." Quite to the contrary, he devotes the attention he does in the second lecture to T. S. Eliot's touchstones explicitly in order to illustrate the force of change and, in this signal instance, the quirky and distorting individual sensibility that colored Eliot's readings of the canonical texts. As Guillory himself aptly puts it, Eliot's "touchstones are little idiosyncratic canons, just what canons are not supposed to be."

The principal topic of debate in the exchanges here is pleasure. Perhaps this is inevitable because the kinds of pleasure afforded by the reading of a work of literature, as against the kind of pleasure one gets from a glass of sherry, may be ultimately resistant to description and definition. In any case, Kermode has chosen to approach the subject of literary pleasure episodically and ruminatively rather than systematically, concluding with an example from Wordsworth that proves to be suggestive but not altogether transparent, and as a consequence his respondents variously understand what he means by pleasure, with a certain amount of speaking at cross-purposes with one another that is common in such discussions. I can hardly pretend to offer a grand synthesis of what pleasure in literature entails, but I would like to attempt some sorting out of a couple of the issues raised.

John Guillory argues energetically for a kind of democracy of pleasures and is unhappy with what he takes to be an argument for a "higher pleasure" in the reading of literature in Kermode's first lecture. Behind this objection, I suspect, lies a certain nervousness that Kermode, as a critic raised under the old literary dispensation, may want to haul us back to the antediluvian era when Matthew Arnold and many in his footsteps claimed a "higher authority" (Guillory's phrase) for literature as a kind of secular substitute for revealed religion. In fact, Kermode does not himself speak of "higher pleasure" (though the phrase occurs in a quotation he offers from Wordsworth), only of a specific and rather peculiar pleasure in the reading of canonical works, which is precisely what Guillory argues for, nor does he associate this pleasure with the idea of authority. It is by no means necessary to assume a hierarchy of pleasures in order to recognize that there is something different about the pleasure afforded by a great work of literature. Even a distinction between simple and complex pleasures is not entirely helpful in this regard. The pleasure of a hot shower is no doubt simpler than the pleasure of reading Proust, but it is not self-evident that, say, the pleasure of sexual consummation, especially when an intense relationship between the partners is involved, is less complex than the reading experience, though it is surely quite different in kind.

The precise nature of the difference remains elusive. Kermode early on invokes the notion of the Czech structuralist Jan Mukařovský that "part of the pleasure [of the literary work] and the value its presence indicates and measures is likely to lie in the power of the object to transgress, depart, interestingly and revealingly, from the accepted ways of such artifacts." Although this concept does not then become a central part of the argument, it might well be retained as one useful point of departure. A canon, after all, constitutes itself as a trans-historical community of texts, and it lives its cultural life through a constant dynamic interplay between each new text and an unpredictable number of antecedent texts and formal norms and conventions. As Kermode notes at the beginning of the second lecture, "Each member [of the canon] exists only in the company of others; one member qualifies or nourishes another." In a related line of thought, Carey Perloff properly reminds us that it is writers, resuscitating and transforming and interacting with their predecessors, who both perpetuate and modify the canon, not professors or critics compiling lists of approved authors. This impulse of innovation or even, as Kermode proposes, of transgression within a community of admired predecessors may distinguish the pleasure of the text from at least the simpler kinds of extraliterary pleasures. If you enjoy a hot shower after exercise, you might be disconcerted by a noticeable alteration in the water pressure or temperature. If you are an admirer of the novels of Philip Roth, you certainly don't want *Sabbath's Theater* to give you exactly the same pleasure you experienced in reading *The Counterlife* or a novel by anybody else, and its utterly surprising fusion of obscenity, hilarity, and somber existential seriousness is innovative and transgressive in precisely the way that Kermode, paraphrasing Mukařovský, suggests a literary work should be.

But if some sort of purposeful novelty, together with a necessary affirmation of belonging to the existing textual community, points to the defining context of the pleasure of the canonical work, what is its differential character, its special tenor? In regard to this central question, the discussion gets a little murky on all sides. Guillory, reasonably enough, wants us to keep in mind the specificity of the pleasure we experience through literature, but he himself makes no proposal as to what that might be. Hartman, who in contrast to the other discussants is uneasy with the very association of pleasure and canon, worries that the term and concept of pleasure "glides over the abyss." He offers no more than an oblique intimation of what this might mean, though he appears to be reacting to the introduction into the discussion by Kermode of Roland Barthes's notion of *jouissance* with its suggestion of a response so intense that it shatters identity.

French theorists have often exhibited a certain predilection for arresting and metaphysically violent overstatement, and Hartman's horror of the abyss that is opened up through the concept of pleasure may be tinged by such habits of thought. Kermode, here as throughout his work, expresses a more measured (perhaps British) sensibility, but he may nevertheless be retaining a vestige of Barthes's vocabulary of ontological crisis when, as he considers his Wordsworthian prooftext, he proposes a conjunction of happiness and dismay as the distinctive character of the pleasure derived from reading a canonical text. The element of dismay or loss certainly sets off reading from rope dancing and sherry, and I suppose it is meant here to be part and parcel of the "philosophical" character of canonical literature, on the assumption that any philosophical reflection on the human condition is bound in some way to recognize ineluctable loss, dissolution, and the painful disjunction between human aspirations and the arbitrary circumstances of existence. The intertwining of happiness with dismay certainly covers a lot of ground in canonical literature. It works aptly enough in "Resolution and Independence," and it is surely evident in a wide range of texts from the Book of Job to *King Lear* to *Moby-Dick* and *The Brothers Karamazov*. In reading such works, we feel a keen sense of exhilaration in the magisterial power (and the courage) of the poetic imagination together with a wrenching experience of anguish over the vision of suffering or gratuitous evil or destructiveness articulated in the work. Hartman is surely right to link this peculiar combination with what in other conceptual frameworks is called the *sublime*.

The obvious problem is that not all canonical works are expressions of the sublime. Two large categories of literature that include many eminent canonical texts have very little to do with the sublime and cannot be linked with the experience of loss or dismay except by a long interpretive stretch. The first, which is manifested in certain kinds of novels, satiric poetry, and drama, is a worldly literature of the quotidian. In this sort of writing, authors address the web of social institutions, usually contemporary, and the spectrum of types of character, with their sundry foibles and virtues, who can be seen colliding and interacting within these social contexts. Intelligence of observation is encouraged by such texts and is essential to the pleasure of reading them, and this exercise of intelligence is inseparable from the writer's deft management of literary form—style, narrative invention, dialogue, strategies for the complication of meaning through irony, and so forth. Among the most striking examples of this literature of worldliness in English are the poetry of Alexander Pope—one might think especially of his remarkable "Moral Essays"—and the novels of Jane Austen. The pleasure afforded by such writing is a particularly adult sort of pleasure (which is not to say "higher") that is social and moral rather than philosophical. It involves no dissolution of the self nor an existential abyss but a delighting play of perception, an invitation to ponder motives and make subtle discriminations about behavior, character, and moral predicaments.

As a pleasure of the faculty of intelligence enacted through the medium of artful language, it is distinguished from extraliterary pleasures, whether simple or complex. Sometimes, this worldly perspective may be prominent in a literary work that also expresses loss or dismay, as in Stendhal or Proust, but that is not necessarily the case.

The other category of literary expression that is for the most part removed from the sublime is comedy. One may grant that there are works in which the comedy makes itself felt as a triumph over loss and which thus seem to correspond to Kermode's description of a mingling of happiness and dismay: in Joyce's *Ulysses* the high-spirited comic play and the grand concluding affirmation of love and life are brave assertions in the face of the disaster of the Blooms' marriage, the remembered death of their infant son, and the decline of Leopold Bloom's manhood; in Sterne's *Tristram Shandy* the endlessly amusing wit and sheer farce are in part a nervous response to fears of impotence, castration, and the menace of death by consumption that pursues the narrator. Many instances of comic literature, however, are untinged by such anxieties. The fiction of Rabelais, some though not all of the plays of Molière, and in the biblical canon itself the Book of Esther (a fusion of folktale and satiric farce) give pleasure through the high exuberance of verbal and narrative invention. *Tom Jones* is another case in point: the protagonist's temporary banishment from Paradise Hall, the shadow of possible incest and imprisonment, cannot be taken very seriously within the comic framework of the novel, which constantly delights through the subtle exercise of witty irony and the inventive deployment of amusing incidents and human types. If literature, as all the participants in the present discussion variously assume, involves some sort of grappling with the multifarious aspects of the human condition, including the most deeply troubling ones, it is also a form of play with language, story, and represented speech, and the playfulness itself, exhibited by a master of the medium, may give us, creatures that we are of language, story, and speech, abiding pleasure of a sort that makes us want to retain such works in a canon.

The neglect of playfulness may be a symptom of our somber intellectual climate. There is no place for it, for example, in Harold Bloom's *The Western Canon*, which sees the canonical in terms of constant struggle and confrontation, and though there are no Bloomians among the discussants here, they seem to share his sense that literature is an existentially serious business, and they do not allow much room for the possibility that the pleasure of the canonical text might also sometimes be unserious or even "low" (though perhaps at the same time complex).

The purview of this discussion of the canon is of course academic, but that may be something of a problem because no vocational group I can think of is more inclined than the scholarly one to confuse the contours of its professional world with the contours of the world. Thus, Hartman wonders why "the change in the study of literature, registered and regretted by Kermode, is uncanonical," whereas what is uncanonical surely should pertain to the works of literature themselves, not to the attitudes and methods that are brought to bear on the analysis of literature in our institutions of higher learning, and I don't think Kermode means to suggest that literary studies have become "uncanonical," only that they have developed some odd views of what makes a canon. A syllabus or a list of required readings for a particular degree is a very definite thing set out by academic authority, but professors often confound what they do on campus with the workings of cultural or even political reality beyond the perimeter of the campus.

In this regard, Carey Perloff's intervention provides a welcome corrective to the general discussion. Perloff, not a scholar but the artistic director of San Francisco's American Conservatory Theater, offers a perspective from the frontline where old works are pre-served or revived for living audiences and where new ones begin to make their way into the canon. From this practical vantage point, she sees the canon shaped and redirected by artists seeing anew and freshly using the work of other artists, without professorial mediation. Her view of the canon is a hopeful one, not darkened by existential brooding, because she is a witness to how its life is repeatedly renewed by the creative energy of individual artists conscious of their predecessors, and one may assume that her notion of the pleasure conveyed by canonical works is quite concrete because if the pieces she puts on the stage did not give pleasure to their audiences, she would be out of a job.

Pleasure, then, does prove to be one reasonably serviceable criterion for the canonical, though as these exchanges indicate, it has its ambiguities. One does not want to claim, as I suspect all the discussants would agree, that this pleasure of the canonical is associated with some unique authority inhering in canonical texts. Literature pleases in part because it invites us to see through the resources of language more subtly or more profoundly who we are and what our world is like, and that vision may be dismaying or delightful or both. There are, of course, other ways of seeing that may have their own profundities. Whatever its subject, mood, and form, literature also pleases because we experience delight or exultation in witnessing the exercise of sheer word-magic and the architectonic mastery of the imagination. When works once valued cease to please as times and tastes change, they slip to the margins of the canon—as, say, has happened with the novels of George Meredith or the poetry of James Thomson. Pleasure in reading, of course, is not purely aesthetic nor purely the consequence of the formal properties of the text and is often colored by the values articulated in the work. The evolution of the canon thus cannot be explained solely in terms of the intrinsic qualities of the literary texts but must also be linked to rather complicated considerations of social and cultural history, as Kermode's notion of change intimates. Such considerations, however, would carry us beyond the horizon of the discussion gathered in this volume, which at least provides some glimmerings of illumination on a question that is urgent for our culture.

Pleasure and Change

FRANK KERMODE

Pleasure

In the course of this talk I shall have to try to explain how pleasure can enter into a discussion of canons. That is one purpose of this first talk, and if I achieve it I should have no trouble getting Shakespeare into the argument in my second talk. The real difficulty is that the topic of the canon is not in itself an obvious source of delight, and the enterprise may challenge the speaker's power to achieve that perception of likeness in dissimilars so admired by Aristotle. Moreover, the job will need to be done without the tedium involved in going too closely over ground, making or refuting points in a way with which we have all grown too familiar of late.

There was a time when discussion of canons was angry but simple in the manner of Dr. Leavis: should Milton be dislodged, or Shelley saved from demotion to the apocrypha? These arguments were keenly, even passionately, conducted, but beneath them was a general agreement that getting the canon right was a social issue, though determined by aesthetic argument; it was rarely or never suggested that the entire canon, whatever its members, should be decanonized. The debate turned on such matters as Milton's grand style or Shelley's reprehensible vagueness. It was more or less silently abandoned when such considerations had come to seem chimerical; the real questions being whether the notion of canon wasn't a wicked myth, designed to justify the oppression of minorities—a political propaganda weapon now at last revealed as such and, as the word goes, "demystified." Questions of literary value were for the most part set aside as without relevance or even derided as demonstrable nonsense.

By a series of institutional decisions, a very large number of people of whom it might be said that they are paid to do the community's serious reading for it, ceased to talk much about literature, sometimes dismissing the notion that there was really any such thing, and inventing new things to talk about, for instance, gender and colonialism. These matters being beyond question urgent, it seemed natural to stop discussing literature as such, except when it seemed profitable to deny its existence. Criticism, as formerly understood, suffered in company with its subject, and the experts moved easily up to what, if you approved, you might call a metacritical level.

Under the older dispensation, one might choose between several critical methodologies which had in common only the assumptions that it was permissible to speak of literary quality and that one could read with a degree of attention that warranted the issuing of judgments, even of declarations, that some works demanded to be read by all who claimed the right to expound and instruct. Under the newer metacritical dispensation, there were now many interesting ways of banning such activities and substituting for them methods of description and analysis which might derive their force from linguistics, politics, anthropology, psychoanalysis, or what were claimed to be brand-new, unillusioned, and exciting ways of writing history.

Having grown old, it has been my inescapable fate to live and work under both dispensations. I have written about canons, and about many other things, with double vision and tried to take part in controversies of both kinds—the old one about dislodgment or insertion, the new one about the canon as an abuse of power. And as Chateaubriand said in the *Mémoires d'Outretombe*, "If I compare the two terrestrial globes, the one I knew at the beginning of my life and the one I now behold at the end of it, I no longer recognize the one in the other."[1]

The great turning point, as most would agree, occurred in the sixties, when I was already in my forties, an age at which it is

---

[1] Quoted in Lionel Gossman, *Between Literature and History* (Cambridge, Mass.: Harvard University Press, 1990), 383.

thought to be difficult to change one's whole way of thinking about literature or anything else. Although unhappy about this generalization, I am far from believing that I can look back and discern a clear trajectory of belief—say, of conversion, apostasy, reconversion to a reformed faith. Muddle there must be, and what I have to say in these lectures will almost certainly confirm its presence in my head. But I imagine almost everybody in the business, a few fanatics apart, would admit to some degree of muddle. It is a function of time's passage; it must follow from the changing demands of an institution. The very new is exciting, its proponents invested at least momentarily with charisma. But there follows the well-known declension from the charismatic to the institutional, whereupon out of the resulting discontent there is generated a new charisma, detected and espoused by loyal expositors, while, down below in the graduate schools, a paradigm always likely to be slightly out of date prevails.

Fashions succeed one another rapidly (Pierre Cardin once defined *fashion* as "that which goes out of fashion"), and work that was for a while unchallenged (as to its importance, though not as to its detail)—Leavis, Frye, Blackmur—drops out of view more or less completely. Now and again somebody like Christopher Norris may, in a pious moment, attempt to "recuperate" a particularly brilliant old-style reputation by claiming its owner as a New New Critic *avant la lettre*—Empson in this case, now to be thought of as having, in his "great theoretical summa," *The Structure of Complex Words*, anticipated deconstruction. The grumpy old man repudiated this notion with his habitual scorn, calling the work of Derrida (or, as he preferred to call him, "Nerrida") "very disgusting," though showing little sign of having attended to any part of it.

I have a notion about the course of intellectual history which tries to take into account the operation of chance. Freud simply ignored Dilthey and Saussure: how might his work have differed had he read either of them? I. A. Richards got his psychology from the doctrines prevailing in the Cambridge of his day, from Stout and Ward and William James, with some neurological stiffening from Sherrington. He knew Wittgenstein personally but did not attend to his philosophies. His philosophy master was G. E. Moore, whose authority barely survived the interventions of Wittgenstein. No one could positively say he lacked good teachers, but they closed the door of his attention on Freud. Richards was interested in a huge range of things, including Gestalt psychology, and he can hardly, even in the twenties, have avoided all talk of Freud—indeed he is said at one point to have contemplated a career in psychoanalysis—but, as in the case of Wittgenstein, there was no imprint. His course was set. Again, it might have made a difference if he had bothered with Nietzsche, as with his classical background he might well have done; but Nietzsche, I gather, is never so much as mentioned in the large body of Richards's writings.

I mention this example because here was a deeply serious thinker, in a strong position to know what was happening in the world of ideas—especially since the polymathic C. K. Ogden was his early collaborator—but who took his own road and not the one that might have had more interest for a modern audience. My point is that chance, aided by individual formation and the vagaries of personal interest and the interests of interpretive communities, may cause diversions that, in the long run, ensure the total neglect of the road not taken—and this is true of the history of modern literary criticism. Only rarely is anybody ready to return to the fork in the road and take a look down the other path.

One such path, more recent but now, I think, largely abandoned, was formalism—I mean the Eastern European variety that was imported in the sixties under the influence mostly of Tzvetan Todorov and propagated by the example of distinguished émigré authors such as Roman Jakobson, both in his early work, as it belatedly became available, and in his later adventures with Lévi-Strauss and others as an analyst of Baudelaire and Shakespeare.

While I was thinking about the divisions in my own mind and reflecting that aesthetic response—pleasure—has a rather restricted part in modern critical thinking, I remembered a distinction drawn by the Czech critic Jan Mukařovský, who happened to be interested in aesthetic pleasure, not yet a taboo subject. Broadly speaking, he argued that the poetic object might be studied with formalist severity as artifact, but that its aesthetic purpose is achieved only by the action of a responsive reader. This response will certainly be conditioned by the norms and values of the reader's community, but also by individual choices and characteristics—very roughly speaking, by what gives him or her pleasure. Mukařovský further believed that part of the pleasure and the value its presence indicates and measures is likely to lie in the power of the object to transgress, to depart, interestingly and revealingly, from the accepted ways of such artifacts.

Thus, to qualify as possessing an aesthetic function, the work must give pleasure, and it must also be new. Mukařovský believed that such works had value because they gave pleasure to the individual, and were at the same time socially valuable because of the common element in the response of serious readers. The question as to how the work can be expected to stay new—one remembers the point as made by Thomas Love Peacock—is a hard one. But Mukařovský was willing to take account of the changingness in time of poetic works (inevitably so, if only because the storehouse of norms and values is restocked) that continues long after their first serious readers are dead. He did not doubt that aesthetic value changed and might possibly disappear; the important point was that since its source is in the reader, it will in any case be different from one epoch to another. That is an important issue for believers in canonicity, and it is one I shall take up in my second talk. Nowadays, we probably associate approaches to this problem with the work of later writers, notably Hans-Georg Gadamer and perhaps Hans Robert Jauss, though it is also a matter of importance to biblical scholars.

This way of talking has an advantage denied to the anglophone variety of formalism with its now universally deplored emphasis on the autotelic virtues of a poem, for it can deal with pleasure without neglecting the relations between art and society. Unlike some other familiar theories, it ascribes the power of the social link to the aesthetic efforts of individuals. More of that later. For the moment, it is enough to say that Mukařovský thought that the poetic work, considered in its aesthetic aspect, had the power to give pleasure, and to continue to do so even though responses, and in a sense the work itself, must also change. Failure to give pleasure breaks the link, because pleasure is the very condition of the individual response. Failure to undergo change harms the work by reducing the pleasure that arises, perhaps can only arise, from modernity, from the process of defamiliarization that is in the first place devised by the artificer and in the second place becomes the work of time.

Having remarked at the outset that pleasure and the canon may seem uneasy bedfellows, I now proceed to argue that they are not necessarily so, that the clash is only apparent. Indeed I hold it to be a necessary though not obvious requirement of the canonical that it should give pleasure. Pleasure, as the legendary Oxford don was recorded as saying, can be a very worrying subject—a further illustration, if one were needed, of the fact that praxis can be more fun than theory. Plato seems to have said that pain was the result of disorder in the organism, pleasure arising from the restitution of order. Being cold is painful; getting warm is pleasant. But there are higher forms of pleasure not involving organic processes: the fear of a painful disturbance is itself painful; the expectation of relief from that fear is pleasant (*Philebus*, 32c). The argument grows complicated but broadly speaking one can say that Plato always thinks of pleasure in relation to a painful want or lack.[2]

---

[2] See, for example, the discussion in A. E. Taylor, *Plato: The Man and His Work* (London: Methuen, 1960), ch. 16.

However, we are now not likely to seek explanations so remote in time. Probably, in setting out to consider this subject, we think first of Freud and his followers. Freud talks about the "pleasure-unpleasure series" and at bottom his argument is based on an idea not altogether dissimilar from Plato's: the activities of the ego cause tensions, the raising of which is felt as unpleasure and their lowering as pleasure.[3] Kenneth Burke's "Psychology and Form" propounds a once-famous theory that literary form consists in creating need (affirming lack) in the reader and then providing the compensatory satisfactions. Peter Brooks thinks the Freudian *eros*, which seeks to combine organic substance into ever-greater unities, drives plot; there is, he argues, "a movement *toward* totalization under the mandate of desire."[4] Thus a lack is eliminated by the conclusion of the plot. But this binding force coexists with its opposite, which seeks to undo connections and destroy—to reduce to an inorganic state. The two instincts interact and "are necessarily present everywhere" (7).

And it is true that whenever one speaks of pleasure, one becomes aware of the many ways in which polarities interact, most simply in the relations of pleasure and pain. It will not be denied that this relationship is often close, and not only in pathological states; the proximity of the pair is a commonplace in love poetry. One remembers Spenser's allegorical Jealousy, for whom "painful pleasure [turns] to pleasing pain" (*Fairy Queen*, III.10.60).

A more modern, more refined view of the matter was proposed by Roland Barthes, in his book *Le Plaisir du texte*. As everybody knows, Barthes distinguished between the pleasures of reading and what he called *jouissance*, a term associated in French with, among other things, orgasm, and connoting an experience not simply pleasant but mixed with something perhaps best described as dismay.

---

[3] For example, in *An Outline of Psychoanalysis* (Hogarth, 1949), 3, 67ff.

[4] *Reading for the Plot: Design and Invention in Narrative* (Cambridge, Mass.: Harvard University Press, 1992), 37.

In the text of *jouissance*, he says, "pleasure, language, culture, are in pieces." This text is "absolutely intransitive, the extreme of perversion." The experiences of pleasure and *jouissance* are not always sharply distinguished, for they can occur together, but the text of *jouissance* always involves a loss, a dispersion; it is outside the context of pleasure, is indeed closer to pain.[5] The experience in question is beyond the scope of descriptive criticism, for such commentary would have to be of the nature of *jouissance* itself, a desperate, crazed plagiarism amounting to "une grande perte subjective" (93) quite different in quality from the obsessive repetition of the text of pleasure, which, in its very nature, requires some form of social participation. As Stephen Heath expresses it, pleasure arises from a link with "cultural enjoyment and identity," whereas *jouissance* shatters that identity and is not to be identified with enjoyment.[6]

I want now to talk about Wordsworth and about a particular poem I have often discussed before, as many members of this audience must have had to do. Certain aspects of this poem seem to me to be illuminated by the Barthesian pairing—*plaisir* and *jouissance*—and in this respect I believe it resembles a good many other canonical poems. Wordsworth, it will be remembered, set enormous store by pleasure, regarding it as essential to poetry and to poets and always fearing its diminution in himself, and consequently a progressive failure to supply it to others. He said that the poet "writes under one restriction only, the necessity of giving immediate pleasure to a human Being possessed of that information which may be expected of him"—not as a lawyer, a physician, and so on, but "as a Man."[7] That is to say, the pleasure of the individual could be related to the response expected from

[5] *Le Plaisir du texte* (Paris: Editions du Seuil, 1973), 37–38.

[6] Barthes, *Image-Music-Text*, edited and translated by Stephen Heath (New York: Hill and Wang, 1977), introduction.

[7] Preface to *Lyrical Ballads* (1802), in *Selected Poems*, edited by J. O. Hayden (London: Penguin, 1994), 443.

a citizen of ordinary formation—an educated public. Wordsworth was keen to distinguish this pleasure from any to be derived, as he put it, from rope dancing or sherry, the point being that poetry was not only a source of pleasure, it was philosophical. In the world as it was, "a multitude of causes, unknown to former times, are…acting with a combined force to blunt the discriminating powers of the mind, and unfitting it for all voluntary exertion to reduce it to a state of almost savage torpor" (438). How easy, then, to lose that higher pleasure, when a man is rightly "pleased with his own passions and volitions" (441) and can expect other men to feel the same. A taste for rope dancing and sherry can outlive the philosophical pleasures of the poet. Incidentally, that could only be achieved or maintained by efforts of great originality, by new defamiliarizing ways of writing poetry, as Wordsworth announced in his 1800 preface. The effort was great, and so was the effort to rediscover the power to supply these needs, and although it can itself be a principal theme of poetry, loss of power and the fear of that loss are sources of dismay, as Coleridge would also testify, and Yeats, too.

The conjunction of pleasure and dismay is a well-known feature of Romantic lyric poetry, and it can be bewildering to criticism, which is far more at ease with pleasure than its senior partner—in a sense its opposite as well as its complement—*jouissance*. The prose of Wordsworth has nothing to say concerning the dismay that is the shadow of pleasure, perhaps because, as Barthes believed, it is impossible to write *about* it. But the poetry certainly speaks a good deal of loss and dismay.

"Resolution and Independence" is an archetypal Romantic poem with a powerful influence on the future of the art. Yet it remembers anterior poetry, deferring to it with its rhyme royal, the stanza of *Troilus and Criseyde* and *The Rape of Lucrece*, though with the last line a Spenserian alexandrine, a device used by Chatterton in his "Excellent Ballad of Charity." The stanza is traditionally associated with narrative, but this is in its peculiar way a narrative, though highly original, like no narrative poem before it except some of Wordsworth's own, though quite like some that came after it.

I have tried more than once to say something interesting, something reflecting my own permanent interest, in this poem. It is very naive to begin by saying what one takes it to be about, or what it isn't about, but one must start somewhere, so we may begin by annoying many modern Wordsworthians by saying it is really less about the poverty of the leech gatherer (a man "traveling alone among the mountains and all lonely places, carrying with him his own fortitude and the necessities which an unjust state of society has entailed upon him") than about the prospect of the poet's poverty, the blank fear of "a young poet...overwhelmed by the thought of the miserable reverses that have befallen the happiest of men, viz. Poets." The plot of the poem, as you recall, is thus: the poet experiences joy in a beautiful morning landscape, runs with the hare in her mirth, escapes his melancholy thoughts of the previous night, but suddenly the mood changes, and it is as if such a change was the necessary consequence of joy:

As high as we have mounted in delight
In our dejection do we sink as low.

The poet is then plunged into "dim sadness, and blind thoughts I knew not nor could name." He reflects on a life he has "lived in pleasant thought" but adds that though given so much, he has given nothing in return. But this point, emphasizing the early happiness of the poet, seems less important than the premonition of the eventual cost of that vocation, the loss of that happiness:

We poets in our youth begin in gladness;
But thereof comes in the end despondency and madness.

What the narrative has to do is bring together an image of present poverty and the fear of poverty—leeches have become hard to find, and poems are likely to do likewise. And the old man loses his original outline; at first he looks as if he bears "A more than human weight," but soon he is perceived as dissolving into little more than a cloud, a spectral figure. The conversation that follows establishes the man's trade, but his voice, though dignified much as Wordsworth's preface said the language of such speakers should be, fades as his image fades; he is no more than a dream, and the poet in this dream returns to his reflection on "mighty poets in their misery dead." So the poet and the poem are at once troubled by the shape and speech of the man—as if this apparition were a nascent poem, therefore an index of joy, but joy blended with the dread of the misery to come. The poem ends as the poet cheers himself up by saying the brave old man will be an example to him as his powers and his courage fade.

Wordsworth himself insisted, in that strangely agitated letter to Sara Hutchinson, that the poem is about "a young poet... overwhelmed by the thought of the miserable reverses that have befallen the happiest of men, viz. Poets" and about the "interposition of Providence" that gave him a measure of resolution and independence, the strength to contemplate a future poverty. But that is not the whole story. The turning point of the poem (though not of the real encounter from which it took its origin) is precisely the intervention of that "peculiar grace," the "leading from above" that brought him into conversation with the leech gatherer.

These expressions—"peculiar grace," "a leading"—have a strong Calvinist ring, more apposite to the "grave livers," one of whom he takes the old man to be, than to his own. The old man's way of speaking is "above the reach / Of ordinary men" by reason of its stately purity—and in this not unlike the poet's but with different ethical and spiritual foundations. Poets may say, "By our own spirits are we deified," a claim repugnant to grave livers. The two expressions of inspiration, secular and religious, are brought close together for contrast. The stony steadfastness of the old man, the grave liver, is quite another matter from the excited action of the poetic spirit, and the contrast hints at the pain of the more secular type of election.

A "peculiar grace" is a grace vouchsafed freely to a particular person, and here it is applied to the poet, by an intelligible analogy; but he still thinks about the price of it, the cost of achieving the state of grace that makes for poetry and joy, a state from which he may fall; so that the condition of poetry is rather like that of the religious, of Cowper for example, who knows what that state is but dreads and suffers its end.

That is a kind of beginning, but it leaves everything to be said. What, then, ought one to say about this strange and sometimes apparently rather absurd poem, solemn but plainly subject, as Lewis Carroll noticed, to parody? Many interpretations directly convert the poem into material for biography: for example, Stephen Gill regards it as a response to Coleridge's "Letter to Sara Hutchinson," a confrontation of "the introverted defeatism" of that poem.[8] Kenneth R. Johnston detects "a bard very much worried about his staying power," experiencing "a vocational crisis" and seeking to avoid the excesses of Chatterton and Burns as well as the "irresponsibilities" of Coleridge. Whereas Coleridge at the time of the poem was lamenting a broken marriage, Wordsworth had resolved "his failed past romantic history" and was on the point of contentedly marrying Mary Hutchinson.[9] John Worthen in his recent composite biography points out that we can't be sure whether Wordsworth's poem was written after Coleridge's or before it. For him, both poems are part of a protracted "brotherly conversation" between the poets, but in either case he feels it wasn't much use offering the example of the leech gatherer's firm mind, or the reflection that many people were worse off than he was, to

[8] *William Wordsworth: A Life* (New York: Oxford University Press, 1989), 200–202.

[9] *The Hidden Wordsworth* (New York: Norton, 1998), 775–76.

Coleridge, considering the fix he was in; though he does point out that Coleridge published his poem on Wordsworth's wedding day, "as if to say 'this—unfortunately—is true for me, whatever else— luckily for you, is true for *you.*'"[10]

The biographical Coleridge connection is of course very strong, and it is very unfortunate. What ought to matter is the poem itself, as Wordsworth would have agreed. In his letter to Sara, the poet is defending the poem in a quite agitated manner: "if it is not more than very well [after the introduction of the old man] it is very bad, there is no intermediate state." Sara had not liked the figure of the leech gatherer; he wants her to admire him, but more important he insists that the encounter, the peculiar grace, that rescued him from dejection and despair was "almost as an inter-position of Providence," but the poem could only be evidence of that if it was a good, indeed a very good, poem.

The 1815 preface explains what it needed to be—what the figure of the old man and the whole poem needed to be—to satisfy him. Wordsworth was now sure it was very good indeed, so he could use it to illustrate the way imagination operates on "images in a con-junction by which they modify each other." He chooses the lines beginning "As a huge stone is sometimes seen to lie / Couched on the bald top of an eminence" and goes on to the comparisons with the sea beast and the cloud:

The stone is endowed with something of the power of life to approximate it to the sea-beast; and the sea-beast stripped of some of its vital qualities to assimilate the stone; which intermediate image is thus treated for the purpose of bringing the original image, that of the stone, to a nearer resemblance to the figure and condition of the aged man.

I mention this not as a bit of biography, the poet's reading of his own poem, but as an example of the sort of struggle even a very

---

[10] *The Gang: Coleridge, the Hutchinsons & the Wordsworths in 1802* (New Haven, Conn.: Yale University Press, 2001), 189–90.

good critic must take on if he wants to say something useful about a great poem.

Wordsworth is talking, in as clear a way as it is reasonable to expect, as a critic of the poem, trying to explain its internal coalescences and divagations. If the poem is not very good, it must be very bad. In the letter to Sara, he does say something about how he came to write it, but his concern is always with the poem. And of course he says nothing about its relation to Coleridge's dejection. The biographical guesses have their own interest, but it is not the interest of the poem.

What concerns Wordsworth in the letter is what he calls "the feeling of spirituality or supernaturalness" induced by the old man.[11] The mystery, that is, is the mystery not of the old man but of the poem itself. To reduce the poem to autobiography is a policy that not only makes it less interesting but actually makes a worse mistake, by diverting the attention of the reader and so cutting off his relation with the power and the complex pleasures of the work. It explains nothing about the poem's supernaturalness, its powerfully *unheimlich* quality: the identification of the poem itself with a peculiar grace, the conjunctions and disjunctions of pleasure, and *jouissance*. At the end, the old man's poverty is unchanged, and there is nothing the poet can do with his own except hope to endure it, perhaps finding a poem as the old man finds leeches, by perseverance. The gloom is not dispersed by the prayer at the end:

"God," said I, "be my help and stay secure";
I'll think of the Leech-gatherer on the lonely moor!

Curiously, this resignation, this willingness to identify with loss and dissolution, must be thought a constituent of the emotion Wordsworth called "joy." Again and again we find in the best of the poetry a curious blend of delight and dismay.

---

[11] The letter refers to an earlier version of the poem, but the point is not affected.

It seems to me that the integral experience results from some juxtaposition or collision of pleasure and dismay. In a very similar way, the most remarkable lines in the "Immortality Ode" concern

those obstinate questionings
Of sense and outward things,
Fallings from us, vanishings;
Blank misgivings of a creature
Moving about in worlds not realized...

The Wordsworth who wrote those lines was the poet Blake placed among the real poets, the poets among whom "there is no competition," the poet whose best work made Blake feel ill, whose line "But there's a tree, of many one," we learn from Crabb Robinson's *Reminiscences* (1869), 27 February 1852, "threw him almost into a hysterical rapture." We notice that the passages that so disturb Blake are about loss: the loss of the visionary gleam, the way in which the single tree, the single field, "speak of something that is gone." Those were the dismayed monosyllables that gave Blake the experience of combined ecstatic pleasure and dismay.

I understand that I am talking about the poem as if ignorant of such subtle accounts as those of David Bromwich in his *Disowned by Memory*, which place man at the center of the poet's interest. In a different critical dialect, Bromwich remembers those fallings from us, vanishings, and he asks, Why does Wordsworth press upon us these aberrant choices of subject and feeling? It was the question Sara Hutchinson asked when she could not see why so much absorbed attention was given to the leech gatherer. Dorothy wrote back: "when you feel any poem of his to be tedious, ask yourself in what spirit it was written." Very good advice! Bromwich finds in the poem qualities observed there by Arthur Symons ninety years earlier. Wordsworth, said Symons, "has gathered up all his qualities, dignity, homeliness, meditation over man and nature, respectful pity for old age and poverty, detailed observation of natural things, together with an imaginative atmosphere which melts, harmonises, the forms of cloud and rock and pool and the voices of wind and man into a single composition."[12] Well said, but I think too calmly said; Bromwich, less calm, knows about the transgressive unease of the work, an unease which is also relevant to the poet's understanding of man, of nature, and of human life.[13] We feel it in all of Wordsworth's solitaries, "The Old Cumberland Beggar" and the ghostly soldier in the *Prelude* (iv.192–254) from whom the poet departs "with quiet heart." Then there is the narrator in *The Ruined Cottage* who, having heard Margaret's sad tale, leaves her and walks along his road "in happiness" (*The Ruined Cottage*, 525). The bleakness of these lives engenders no conventional lament because, by a peculiar grace, pleasure and loss are coactive in the creation of joy.

Like Blake, we can charge Wordsworth with many faults, but when reading these passages one echoes his more enthusiastic judgments. It is as difficult a critical assignment as can be imagined to explain why delight is so intense, why it is reasonable to say, with Blake, that such writing is "in the highest degree imaginative and equal to any poet but not superior." To speak of pleasure alone does not seem enough, though pleasure, and the possibility of its repeated disappointment and satisfaction, is one key to canonicity.

Perhaps one could analyze "Resolution and Independence" along the lines proposed by Kenneth Burke—considering its artifice, as he brilliantly considers the artifice of the opening scene of *Hamlet*: "We have been waiting for a ghost, and get, startlingly, a blare of trumpets. And, once the trumpets are silent, we feel how desolate are these three men waiting for a ghost, on a bare 'platform'" (29). Burke considers the way music can "deal minutely in frustrations and fulfillments of desire" (36). Or one

---

[12] *The Romantic Movement in English Poetry* (New York: Dutton, 1909), 88. I owe this reference to Professor John Stokes.

[13] *Disowned by Memory* (Chicago: University of Chicago Press, 1998), 137.

could cite Proust on the coexistence of happiness, or of happiness
deferred, with that sense of dismay, even of vastation, that seems
inseparable from it, as in the pages on Venice: as Tony Tanner
expressed it, Ruskin made Venice "not just beautiful but, effec-
tively, *the* site of the Beautiful—the essence realized, the absolute achieved. As such it is almost impossible, unbearable to
contemplate....It is a beauty that both awakens *and*—should it
turn its Medusa face—devastates all desire," as indeed it does after
the departure of Marcel's mother.[14]

It goes without saying that the literature I have referred to is
canonical literature. It is clearly not so on account of its collusion
with the discourses of power; indeed Wordsworthians have to
distinguish between the large proportion of his work that may be
said to do that, and the work that enters into Blake's realm where
there is no competition, where the transaction is first between the
poem and a reader and then, necessarily, between the poem and
many readers, those who, in Wordsworth's words, qualify as human
beings possessed of that information which may be expected of
them, a possession he seems to identify with the possession of true
humanity.

However, it is "by our own spirits" that we are deified and so
able to claim the power to confer upon strings of words or notes or
patches of paint—mere objects—the honor of being what we call
art. We would hardly do so if the objects, however grim, however
dismaying, did not give us pleasure. Moreover we make lists,
canons, of what we decide is valuable, and these, in the interests of
that humanity, we may press on other people, our successors.
Some of the reasons we give for doing so may be false or self-
serving, or at any rate fallible. But the cause is a good one. And
pleasure is at the heart of it. So is change; but of that, more later.

---

[14] *Venice Desired* (Oxford: Blackwell, 1992), 230.

Change

The great statue of the general Du Puy
Rested immobile, though neighboring catafalques
Bore off the residents of its noble Place....

There never had been, never could be, such
A man. The lawyers disbelieved, the doctors

Said that as keen, illustrious ornament,
As a setting for geraniums, the General,
The very Place Du Puy, in fact, belonged

Among our more vestigial states of mind.
Nothing had happened because nothing had changed.
But the General was rubbish in the end.

There are those who would take Wallace Stevens's general as an allegory of the canon, which they have been known to describe as a set of obsolete, moldering monuments. However, the statue in this case has not moldered; nothing has happened; the statue's greatness is merely monumental and immobile; nothing has changed except the taste or opinion of the intelligentsia. But this opinion can produce what the poet elsewhere calls "a single text, granite monotony," and it is enough to dismiss the statue as an irrelevant, even contemptible survival, with no power to elicit our attention. It outlives its human neighbors and is probably the worse for that. Nobody talks about it as a work of art, for that would require a particular form of attention and a tradition of attention, however varied in kind, that has been broken off. Without this form of attention, the general is rubbish. Texts too must change, or rather, we must choose to grant them the blessing of change, for that alone will save them from their only other possible fate, namely, to be rubbish in the end. Failing that benediction, equestrian statues, and all other objects of art, belong to vestigial states of mind. The same fate could attend the *Inferno* or *Antony and Cleopatra* if our mind but changed its tune. There are signs that some would like it to do so, though others sometimes succeed in redirecting attention to works that have somewhere, in the course of history, lost interest.

Reception history informs us that even Dante, Botticelli, and Caravaggio, even Bach and Monteverdi, endured long periods of oblivion until the conversation changed and they were revived. Some hope it will continue to say new things about them, that the giant will go on living in change rather than die for the lack of it. Indeed, outside the universities, this group may still be large, remaining sure that although "it must change," the work can still, as it changes, give pleasure.

One consequence of canonicity is that whether the canon is formed by theological fiat or pedagogical authority or indeed chance, each member of it fully exists only in the company of others; one member nourishes or qualifies another, so that as well as benefiting from the life-preserving attentions of commentary, each thrives on the propinquity of all: in a sense all become part of one larger book and all are changed in the process. In this sense, we need to insist with Schleiermacher that acts of interpretation have regard to wholes, not parts. A book inside a canon is a different book from what it would have been outside that canon. This is obviously true of the Bible, interrelations between the parts of which have been traced, invented, and explained by centuries of commentators. Left out of the canon, books may disappear entirely, like the gospels that didn't get in. The Song of Songs might have disappeared, for it was almost excluded from the Hebrew Bible, but it was rescued in the nick of time, and so saved for the Christian Bible also, to become the source of great volumes of subsequent poetry and commentary. Or, as one biblical commentator puts it, had Ecclesiastes been excluded from the Hebrew Bible, as it might well have been, and then, after almost two millennia of neglect, had turned up among the Dead Sea Scrolls, it would be a different book even though the two texts were virtually identical. Even more obviously, the Christian Old Testament is not the same book as the Jewish Bible though in substance it is so, because Christian commentary transformed it in the light of the New Testament, a new covenant, a new deal ensuring a drastic retrospective rewriting that required no textual change.

All this reinforces the proposition that there is an element of chance in canonicity, and many examples testify to the truth of this. We ourselves make canons by attending closely to texts and contexts, but there may be among those texts some we choose not to attend to and which remain there by inertia. Other works may have some claim to be treated as canonical but aren't. Many authors have been rescued from neglect, but there must be many more who have had no such luck. A few plays of Sophocles were saved by an Alexandrian grammarian; Traherne, lost for almost three centuries, turned up in a London bookstall and benefited from the revival of interest in early seventeenth-century poetry that was gaining strength at the time of the discovery. There is no intrinsic preservative, but somebody at some point must have thought these were good things, and so began the history of their success. This person need not be a professional scholar, and very often isn't: the rediscovery of Botticelli was effected by persuasive amateurs (and was often based on paintings that weren't by Botticelli). But once retrieved, the works are kept alive by conversation, eventually supported by serious scholarship.

The retrieval of forgotten music, stimulated no doubt by the compact disc, goes on all the time. Such revivals mark changes in the understanding of the audience and complementary changes in performance. The other day, my interest was caught by a new recording of Handel's opera *Rinaldo*. Back in 1940, I was writing about this opera in a never-to-be published thesis about Aaron

Hill, poet, theater manager, projector or entrepreneur in general, friend of the novelist Richardson, unwanted friend of the poet Pope. Hill was responsible for inducing Handel to write this, the first of his many English operas. Hill himself sketched the libretto, which was hastily translated into Italian by a man called Rossi. As Handel had brought from Italy quantities of music never heard in London and therefore reusable, the collaborators were able to paste everything together in a very short time. The staging was absurdly elaborate and fallible, making much use of machinery, and the leading role was, absurdly in the view of some contemporaries, sung by a famous castrato, Nicolini. The result was apparently even more chaotic than the circumstances and the novelty of the genre might suggest, but the opera was a success, despite the sardonic notices of Addison:

An Opera may be allowed to be extravagantly lavish in its Decorations, as its only Design is to gratify the Senses and keep up an indolent Attention in the Audience. Common Sense however requires that there should be nothing in the Scenes and Machines which may appear Childish and Absurd. (*Spectator*, March 6, 1711)

Addison disliked the real sparrows, meant to inhabit the pasteboard groves on stage, which flew about the theater putting out the candles, while their singing was imitated absurdly by "a Consort of Flageolets." In the view of Addison and others, there was nothing much to be said for Italian opera, with its boring plots, ridiculous conventions, un-English language, and un-English music. Outrageous to common sense, *Rinaldo* nevertheless packed them in. But it disappeared from our eyes and ears for centuries, remembered only when cited as the source of the aria *lascia ch'io pianga*. Sixty years ago, it was almost inconceivable that I or anybody else should ever hear, let alone see, this opera. Now, with luck, one can see it staged, and one can choose between two full CD versions. The scene in which the flageolet and its consorts imitate birdsong is, in spite of Addison, particularly admired. The story is impossible to remember, but it is now recognized as providing scope for some impressive, powerfully pleasing music, of a kind we had, to our cost, ignored for centuries, music very unlike the Handel who kept the attention of our grandfathers with the solemnities of *Messiah* and *Israel in Egypt*.

How explain this change? We have a modern familiarity with the baroque; we have scholars who understand it, and singers and musicians who know how to perform it; we can accommodate the heroic or pathetic gestures, the long recitatives, and the *da capo* arias. Our map of musical history has been redrawn; we have discovered how to listen to this music, a different skill from listening to Mozart or Verdi or Wagner. The change is fueled by more generous notions in ourselves; nothing has happened to the operas except they have come to be understood in their own pleasure-giving terms. They are no longer rubbish, like the general. We have made this music modern by acts of historical understanding; we have changed it and released its power to please. So, the canon expands. Of course, a withdrawal of attention can by the same token contract it.

Changes in the canon obviously reflect changes in ourselves and our culture. It is a register of how our historical self-understandings are formed and modified. At the simplest level, we know about the differences between our own understandings of old texts and the understandings of our predecessors, or even those of contemporaries in disagreement because of generational differences, or contrary political presumptions. We may attribute our grasp of the issue to our superior understanding generally, yet it is just that assumption we are likely to say we feel an urgent need to question if we want to rid ourselves of the historically embedded prejudices that are the main support of our conviction that we are historically privileged.

Issues of this sort first seemed important in the sphere of religion. Everybody knows Schleiermacher's slogan: "The task is to understand the text at first as well as and then better than its author." To achieve this understanding, one was recommended to study "the field of language shared by the author and the original public." The effort called for is philological and its ambition utopian; later students saw the need to incorporate in the relationship the inquirer's own historical situation. As Gerald Bruns puts it in his excellent book, what we now have to ask is "the question of what it is that happens...when we try to make sense of something."[1] The moment of interpretation is now fixed in the present. The emphasis shifts once more to the historical context of the interpreter, his powers and desires and those of his community, and so we see ourselves in the position of Gadamer, who could say that "*verstehen* is less knowing what the text means in itself than it is in knowing how we stand with respect to it in the situation in which we find ourselves."[2] It follows, as he remarks, that we understand differently if we understand at all; an interpretation that merely repeated an earlier one would be false. And this is another way of changing the canon.

Pre-understandings are an important issue. Of course they vary. Gadamer calls them "prejudices":

[A] hermeneutically trained mind must be, from the start, sensitive to the text's quality of newness. But this kind of sensitivity involves neither "neutrality" in the matter of the object nor the extinction of one's self, but the conscious assimilation of one's own fore-meanings and prejudices. The important thing is to be aware of one's own bias, so that the text may present itself in all its newness and thus be able to assert its own truth against one's own fore-meanings.[3]

Of course it isn't easy to be aware of one's own bias, but the reward promised is great: newness. Again, the fact is that it is our

[1] *Hermeneutics Ancient and Modern* (New Haven, Conn.: Yale University Press, 1992), 8.

[2] As expressed by Bruns in ibid., 10.

[3] *Truth and Method* (London: Sheed and Ward, 1975), 238.

job to create that newness. Our way of doing so may be described as "appropriative," meaning only that we have to do something drastic to a canonical text to make it ours, to make it modern.[4] It must be made to answer to our prejudices, and they are necessarily related to the prejudices of our community, even if in reaction to them.

I can't go into the very interesting arguments that have developed on these points, as between the Schleiermachians who seek to inhabit original languages and communities and place each element independently and with historical precision, and those who take Brevard Childs's view, as I do, that the canon is, considered from a different sort of historical point of view, all of a piece and ought not to be split definitively into independent components, as the modern Schleiermachians wish.[5]

Prejudices change like everything else, and they are not consistently held at any particular time, being affected in obvious ways by different levels of communal assumption and doctrinal adhesion. Indeed, as we are all too aware, members of the same institution may hold very different views, have very different prejudices, and none of them may be of much interest to the public at large. Meanwhile, canons are replaced, condemned, or subjected to new commentary. In any case, they change.

Let me now turn to the source of change that at present interests me most. One thing is clear enough from the history of literary criticism, and that is the existence of a discernible consensus as to

---

[4] Bruns, *Hermeneutics*, 76, discusses Brevard Childs's view, arising from the Old Testament, that appropriative understanding is the means by which a text is subjected to a process of "actualization," so that it is not "moored in the past" (*Introduction to the Old Testament as Scripture* [Philadelphia: Fortress, 1979]).

[5] I gave an account of the dispute between Childs and James Barr, the main proponent of the historical view, in "The Argument about Canons," in *The Bible and the Narrative Tradition*, edited by Frank McConnell (New York: Oxford University Press, 1986), 78–96, where I also tried to examine the relevance of the argument to the question of secular canons.

what is worth talking about, whether favorably or not. Certain topics gain sharp definition: modernism, for example, and the general agreement that certain works associated with it are worth intense study, whether approving or dissenting. Modernism is now sunk in the past, and new groups of topics have, by general agreement, supervened. The question as to how these changes come about is doubtless of interest, but I shall speak instead of a more personal element in our responses, responses to individual poems or parts of poems which one may possess or be possessed by, providers of pleasure and dismay.

Most people who care at all about literature have in their heads such poems or parts of poems. It is hard (though not quite impossible) to believe that anybody would want to spend a working life in university departments of literature without having such reserves. But it is a question how communicable the private experience of such works may be. I think Matthew Arnold devised his famous touchstones with some notion of making out of such private experience a set of civilized literary norms acceptable to an educated public. Looking back at the passage in "The Study of Poetry" which sets them forth, one can't help seeing how far short Arnold falls of his stated aim: "to have always in one's mind lines and expressions of the great masters, and to apply them as a touchstone to other poetry." We might expect to find in his selection testimony to a past stage of our culture; bearing in mind the fact and the necessity of change, one would hardly expect the passages to be of eternal validity. What is remarkable and still relevant is that all Arnold needed was a line here and there, sometimes even just a part of a line. There is the address of Zeus to the horses of Peleus in *Iliad* xvii, and that of Achilles to Priam in book xxiv. There are three scraps of Dante and Shakespeare on the ship-boy "upon some high and giddy mast," along with Hamlet's "Absent thee from felicity a while" and some fine fragments of *Paradise Lost*. "If we are thoroughly penetrated by their power," says Arnold, "we shall find that we have acquired a sense enabling us, whatever poetry is laid before us, to feel the degree in which a high poetical quality is present or wanting there."[6]

We might agree that the choices are good bits of poetry, without claiming they have for us the power they evidently had for Arnold. And it isn't easy to understand that power. He says these passages are true and serious—that is what his explanation amounts to. But that seems a rather piffling thing to say about Ugolini's line *Io non piangeva; si dentro impietrai* (*Inferno* xxxiii.49; "I did not weep; inside I turned to stone")—which served perhaps as a reminder of the next words, *piangevan elli*—the children did weep and asked him what was the matter, whereupon he still didn't weep and still didn't answer. And Arnold was remembering, and expecting all educated persons to remember with him, the fate of these children and the pain of what follows: *Lo pianto stesso il pianger non lascia*, where "weeping prevented weeping," where tears were turned back to torment the weeper. In short, the fragment is intended to summon a context of pathos and of ever-increasing and irremediable pain.

The words of Beatrice to Virgil in *Inferno* ii are certainly impressive: *la vostra miseria non mi tange* has, at any rate in isolation from its context, a sort of radiant cruelty: I am so made by God in his grace that "your misery does not touch me." The misery or privation in question is not specifically Virgil's or Dante's but that of the place to which Beatrice descends to help them; yet on its own the remark seems to contrast their wretchedness with her happiness. Dante had, after all, a kind of theological pitilessness; on the gate of hell he inscribes the message that its maker was the high maker, the divine power, *la somma Sapienza e il primo amore* ("the creator of this place of eternal suffering is not only wise but loving"). There is a touch of this quasi-divine indifference in the radiant immunity of Beatrice. The contrast

---

[6] Matthew Arnold, *Selected Essays* (Oxford: Oxford University Press, 1964), 57.

between paradisial content and human misery seems to have appealed to Arnold.

Indeed, abandonment to or at least acceptance of suffering seems to be a characteristic of Arnold's touchstones. The horses of Peleus are weeping at the death of Priam, who was once capable of joy. Milton's Satan is defiant but battered. Ceres' search for her daughter "cost her all that pain." These passages share a somber or stoic quality; Beatrice is there because her exemption from pain emphasizes the plight of all the others. It is hard to see how a large community of readers would find the same intensity of interest in these passages. They are essentially private. All have to do with sorrow; their pleasure arises from their painfulness. It has been pointed out that the Homeric touchstones all come from the *Iliad* and are not even particularly characteristic of that poem as a whole, but "the forces that stirred beneath the surface of Arnold's life find their counterpart in the battle for Troy, the athletic and magnificent figures moving towards death."[7] Arnold loved the Homer of the *Iliad* better than the Homer of the *Odyssey* with its more varied and romantic story, and its final coming home. It provided no touchstone.

So it seems that the touchstone passages, having peculiar connotations of pleasure and pain for Arnold, cannot, for all time and for everybody, bear the broad cultural significance he claims for them. If a culture is involved at all, it must be that of the Victorian professional class, perhaps especially that of men educated at Rugby and Oxford.

T. S. Eliot, the nearest approach to Arnold that a later century could muster, and also one who deplored the contemporary cultural situation, had his own touchstones, though he did not call them that and did not explicitly recommend them for general use. Yet although they are in various ways extremely personal, they

---

[7] Warren D. Anderson, *Matthew Arnold and the Classical Tradition* (Ann Arbor: University of Michigan Press, 1965), 90.

have probably enjoyed more success in literary circles than Arnold's. Some obvious reasons are that they lack the strong ethical coloring of Arnold, are altogether more unexpected, and, at the time of their first exposure, are less familiar. The influence of Eliot has in this as in other respects waned, not least because modes of study now in fashion have little interest in the experience of poetry, which is no longer thought to have much academic or even much cultural relevance.

Yet for the student of poetry, Eliot's touchstones are worth a moment's attention. A favorite source is again Dante, but a rather different Dante. We think of Shakespeare as the source of so many familiar quotations that we sometimes hardly remember their connection with him, and Dante has something of the same familiarity in Italy, except that people seem more aware of the place of famous lines in the poem as a whole. By a memorable chance I once sat in Palermo with Lionel and Diana Trilling at the Christmas Eve dinner table of a Sicilian tour guide, in the company of our host's sons and daughters and their spouses, mostly schoolteachers. Invited to celebrate Dante, Lionel and I dug into our memories and produced mostly lines that had had Eliot's magisterial endorsement: the Paolo and Francesca episode in *Inferno* v, with its extraordinarily tender sensuality: *la bocca me baciò tutto tremante*; the verse adapted or quoted in *The Waste Land*: *ricorditi di me, che son la Pia; / Siena mi fe', disfecemi Maremma*, or *sovegna vos a temps de ma dolor*; and the vanquished hero, now in hell, who ran for the green cloth at Verona and lost, but seemed like one who had won. Others came to mind: the old tailor peering at his needle, and the advice of the doomed Ulysses to his men on the brink of their last voyage: "Consider your inheritance: you were not made to live like beasts but to pursue virtue and knowledge"—incidentally that does sound more Arnoldian, like "in his will is our peace." As we dug out these memories, our mumblings were drowned by the chorus around the table. For this was a company of teachers and to them, these and presumably many other lines of Dante were, quite without their thinking of them as such, touchstones—not ethical guidelines, though some have an ethical or religious tone, and not deliberately memorized but part of the pleasures of their professional habit.

Among the array of fragments, the ones that meant so much to Eliot were, roughly, passages that dealt with seduction, ruin, damnation, and the pains of purgatory. For Eliot, these were also not simply ethical guidelines, though he warmed to their connotations of bold sin (as he discussed it in his essay on Baudelaire) and inevitable punishment; part of Dante's powerful appeal to him was surely a certain theological or moral pitilessness. That eternal torment was ordained by love and wisdom, and that Beatrice was beautifully immune to the pain of the living, were paradoxes that gave him grim pleasure.

Eliot has a special interest in what might be called sexual dismay, and his favorite lines from Dante often bear its mark. It is useful to recall what he said about the reader's surrender to poetry:

You don't really criticize any author to whom you have not surrendered yourself.... Even just the bewildering minute counts; you have to give yourself up, and then recover yourself, and the third moment is having something to say, before you have wholly forgotten both surrender and recovery. Of course the self recovered is never the same as the self before it was given.[8]

This surrender, he believed, was central to the experience of poetry. All will remember the lines from *The Waste Land*:

My friend, blood shaking my heart
The awful daring of a moment's surrender

[8] Letter to Stephen Spender, May 9, 1935, quoted in Spender, "Remembering Eliot," in *T. S. Eliot: The Man and His Work*, edited by Allen Tate (New York: Delacorte, 1966), 55–56.

Which an age of prudence can never retract
By this, and this only, we have existed. (402–5)[9]

And we may also recall these lines from *The Revenger's Tragedy*, made famous and repeatedly cited by Eliot:

Does the silkworm expend her yellow labours
For thee? For thee does she undo herself?
Are lordships sold to maintain ladyships
For the poor benefit of a bewitching minute? (III.v.72–75)[10]

Vindice is addressing the skull of his lover. These famous lines did not start being famous until Eliot said they should be. I have given the text of R. A. Foakes (London, 1966). There is no reason to doubt the correctness of the reading "bewitching minute," but Eliot liked "bewildering," which he found in an edition by J. A. Symonds (1888). Though incorrect, "bewildering" is the stronger reading, as one might say, more modern, more Baudelairean. Eliot made it his own, and "bewildering" introduces into the sexual figure just that element of loss and dismay of which I have spoken. The whole speech of Vindice is a compact of dismay and a sort of ornate disgust. Even the silkworm is undone, spent. And the language is altogether remarkable: for instance, the strange use of "falsify" and "refine," which Eliot had in mind when he referred again to the passage in his study of Massinger and spoke of "that perpetual slight alteration of language, words perpetually juxtaposed in new and sudden combinations, meanings perpetually *eingeschachtelt* into meanings which evidences a very high development of the senses, a development of the English language which we have perhaps never equaled.... Sensation became word and word was sensation."[11] The lines

---

[9] *Collected Poems, 1919–1962* (New York: Harcourt Brace and World, 1963), 68.

[10] *The Revenger's Tragedy*, IIIv.72–75, edited by R. A. Foakes (London: Methuen, 1966), 71.

[11] *Selected Essays* (London: Faber, 1934), 209–10.

demonstrate a close affinity between sexual and poetic *jouissance*, and in substituting "bewildering" for "bewitching," we have a change, an updating, of the passage, to include a darker, more decadent notion of the force of poetry. Here, the late nineteenth-century revival of interest in the Jacobean dramatists has made possible not only new canonical inclusions but also their juxtaposition with the likes of Baudelaire and the other French poets who had won the poet's allegiance. In a still later essay, he decided that "the cynicism, the loathing and disgust of humanity, expressed consummately in *The Revenger's Tragedy*, are immature in the respect that they exceed the object. Their objective equivalents are characters which seem merely to be spectres projected from the poet's inner world of nightmare, some horror beyond words."[12] But this excess was essential to the success of the play. In this essay, Eliot is struggling to justify his view that Tourneur's immaturity could nevertheless have produced a play unsurpassed except by Shakespeare and Marlowe, a play that expresses "an intense and unique and horrible vision of life...to which mature men and women can respond" (189). And it is not without interest that he makes a passing allusion to the other, and inferior, play attributed to Tourneur, *The Atheist's Tragedy*, singling out the line "To spend our substance on a minute's pleasure" (188)—on the same theme as the silkworm passage in the more famous play.

This association of high poetry with sexual pleasure, its concomitant dismay and its subsequent disgust, recurs in other essays on the Jacobean dramatists. Massinger has "masterly construction" but is anemic. Lacking a "nervous system" comparable with Middleton's or Tourneur's or Ford's (211), he inaugurates a period of verse in which the sensibility begins to be dissociated, "the period of Milton," characterized by "a decay of the senses" (210). Milton did not make that surrender to pleasure and dismay, so

---

[12] *Selected Essays*, 189–90.

strong in Tourneur and Middleton. The lines in which De Flores in *The Changeling* refuses Beatrice-Joanna's plea—"Can you weep Fate from its determin'd purpose? So soon may you weep me" (III.iv.162–63) are lines "of which Shakespeare and Sophocles might have been proud,"[13] but it may be that it was the loucheness of the situation enacted that reinforced their appeal. Eliot regards the play as "an eternal tragedy, as permanent as *Oedipus* or *Antony and Cleopatra*,"[14] yet it is the story of an ugly seducer endowed with a language of absolute sexual power. It is surely of interest that when Eliot wanted to reinforce his view of Middleton as a great poet, he chose Beatrice-Joanna's final speech, which contains the marvelous lines "I am that of your blood was taken from you / For your better health" (V.iii.150–51). But Eliot misquotes them: "I that am of your blood," which is weaker and indeed indefensible, losing the idea of bloodletting and making nonsense of her request that they "cast it to the ground regardlessly; / Let the common sewer take it from distinction." He reduces the figure to a mere assertion of blood relationship. The misquotation, involving a loss of sense, is an indication that it was not indeed its plain sense that made it so seductive. Eliot often misquoted lines he admired. In that same final scene, he amazingly changed De Flores's words "I loved this woman in spite of her heart" to "I loved this woman in spite of *my* heart" (1.165). The play he so much admired thus suffered unconscious emendation.

My point is of course to illustrate the process of surrender and incorporation that these alterations suggest. The text changes as the reader changes. It is not too much to say the changes are related to the orgasmic potential of the lines that induced surrender. These authors had to have, were made to have, something of the exemplary modernity of Baudelaire, who said that the unique and

---

[13] *Selected Essays*, 164.
[14] *Selected Essays*, 163.

supreme pleasure of love lies in the certainty of doing ill. "He was at least able to understand that the sexual act as evil is more dignified, less boring, than as the natural, cheery, automatism of the modern world."[15]

So Eliot elevated Middleton and Tourneur to modernity, an essential step toward their preservation. The passages that succeeded in inducing surrender are few, and distinguished from others that might seem to have some claim to inclusion in this personal canon. Eliot liked to combine his admiration for Shakespeare with a few limiting judgments: not as good a technician as Webster, sometimes failing when confronted with Dante. He can be used to put down Milton or Tennyson, but, in Hemingway's expression, he can't go the distance with Dante. In the Dante essay of 1929, Eliot compares the figure, equally admired by Arnold and Yeats, of the old tailor peering at his needle (*Inferno*, xv) with the reaction of Octavius to the dead body of Cleopatra: "she looks like sleep, / As she would catch another Antony / In her strong toil of grace" (V.ii.345–46). All admit the baffling splendor of these lines, but Eliot says that Dante's metaphor tries to make you "see more definitely," while Shakespeare's has an outline less definite but adds to what you see a reminder of Cleopatra's world-changing fascination. I would say he misses something by arguing that Dante observes "rational necessity" and Shakespeare doesn't. If you look at the whole speech of Octavius, you see it begins with some rather clinical observations: Cleopatra's corpse lacks any "external swelling" that would signify poison, and the famous lines, when quoted alone, lack the brilliant moment of surprise as the diagnostic search for symptoms suddenly gives way to the glory. So it is only in a rather guarded way that Eliot makes his surrender. But he returns to Octavius's speech in the Massinger essay, and yet again in his Clark Lectures, this time contrasting it with Dante's lines on Brunetto Latini ("he seemed to be like one

---

[15] *Selected Essays*, 391.

of those who wins, not like him who loses"); and here again Shakespeare's lines, though they show "an image absolutely woven into the fabric of the thought," lack the "*rational* necessity" of Dante's.[16]

Eliot always wanted Dante to win, but it is plain that both of these passages are deep in his imagination, and it is worth remarking that both have to do with punishment and pain. Brunetto and Cleopatra are both sinners and losers on the grand scale, yet both have the air of having won. We may recall that other dazzling moment in Shakespeare's play when Cleopatra, once again for a moment "this great fairy" and the "day o' th' world," greets Antony: "Lord of lords! O infinite virtue, com'st thou smiling from / The world's great snare uncaught?" (IV.viii.17–19)—lines to which most of us surrender, as Auden grudgingly admits when he calls the lines "marvelous," yet recognizing that the marvel comes from the splendor of exultation in the shadow of certain defeat and loss.

The moralizing Auden says that Cleopatra's "strong toil of grace" is the world itself, and "in one way or another it catches us all," even if the snare is grace.[17] Auden introduces religion, Eliot history. They have surrendered and recovered and are trying to think of something to say. Coleridge found the expression "happy valiancy" for such great moments, but explained no better than anybody else the network of responses that invited submission, recovery, and comment. Often what we find to say amounts to no more than an expression of astonishment, which is of little use unless it induces an equivalent submission in our hearers; dull though they may be, they can do this, become part of the

---

[16] *The Varieties of Metaphysical Poetry*, edited by R. Schuchard (London: Faber and Faber, 1993), 123. A better parallel might be the turn at the end of Horace's "Actium Ode" (*nunc est bibendum*...) where Cleopatra, whose defeat is the occasion for the triumphant ode, dies *voltu sereno*, "serene of countenance."

[17] *W. H. Auden: Lectures on Shakespeare*, edited by A. Kirsch (Princeton, N.J.: Princeton University Press, 2000), 238–42.

conversation that prevents such lines from becoming rubbish in the end.

I have been circling 'round my themes: pleasure and change and canon. That the passages I've discussed often have an element of perversity is not surprising; they have to administer shock; they leap out of their context, disrupt it, and cause a kind of delight mingled with dismay. They often, perhaps almost always, defy rational necessity, if only in the most obvious sense; Cleopatra is enormously seductive, but in illustrating that fact for the last time there was no rational necessity for Octavius's sudden glory.

It may be, as Eliot believed, that it is an essential of good poetry that it should, at least on occasion, have an almost prosaic quality, devoid of invitations to emotional surrender, not aiming to achieve one epiphany after another. There must be the *plaisir* that depends on continuities—poetic and social—but it is only from that base that *jouissance* becomes possible. Octavius Caesar, a prosaic figure, examines the body and then issues the great invitation to surrender, in pleasure and dismay. It is, after all, a pattern of experience familiar from ordinary life, which is interrupted by moments that are distinguished from the ordinary run of things and which occupy an intemporal space in our minds, a canon of memories both pleasant and dismaying. They coexist with rational necessities but are clearly distinguished from them, as great poems are from the prose that surrounds them. What is important may be, according to the predilections of each of us, a small thing, a line or two. It might be compared to that little patch of yellow wall in Vermeer's *View of Delft*, which brought Proust's Bergotte to his final and total surrender. However, there was a whole painting, a sober view, containing the patch, and the painting had to be made beautiful by the informed knowledge of those who contemplated it. Proust was already a young man when people began, after more than two centuries of neglect, to look seriously at Vermeer's paintings. They began to give pleasure and, to Bergotte, something like *jouissance* (indeed it could be said that he dies of pleasure), but, before that, informed opinion had to change the canon of painting. So with Hopkins and others; individuals, sharing with others certain powers, change the canon to match their modernity. So a canon changes, and the changes renew the supply of both pleasure and its potent derivative, dismay.

Comments

The Passing of the Canon

GEOFFREY HARTMAN

I am close enough to Frank Kermode's generation to share both its early excitement and later discontent. The excitement came not only from being intimately in touch with the great influx of modernist art, an inexhaustible cornucopia during the first half of the twentieth century, but also from the awareness of a gradual revolution within the study of literature that began in England well before the Second World War. The doors of literary perception were opened, even in the universities, and a heritage, a "cultural capital," as it is now called, began to be more fully disbursed.

Works of art, however, continued to be seen as heroic products. While not above the daily battle, they were survivals of an unaging intellect in a world whose frustrated quest for peace often rested on a vision of the strength of imaginative thought. The literary arts would at once fortify and refine the imagination and be more than a personal good, a vicarious compensation for pain and injustice. Art kept faith alive that there was a place, somewhere on earth and perhaps in every country, as green as Marvell's "green thought in a green shade" and Blake's "And did those feet in ancient time / Walk upon England's mountains green?"

Matthew Arnold was certainly part of this vision of art, and so, despite his stubborn, antiglobal demeanor, was Leavis. The latter's peculiar blend of localism and evangelism, and the touchstone quality of his procedure, helped to foster a new "epoch of concentration" in the study of literature. Counterelitist in spirit, like Ruskin's *Fors Clavigera*, which encouraged workers to discover England's vernacular treasures, this renewal movement added literature to the two books of God "expansed" to the understanding of all in a completion of the Protestant revolution.

What distinguished Leavis from both Ruskin and Arnold was his conviction that the university study of English could counter the pervasive, cultural effects of industrial and technological change. He looked beyond what was moribund in the academy to promote—and I admit something in me still responds to his call— "the university as a focus of consciousness and human responsibility" and "a guarantor of a real performance of the critical function—that critical function which is a creative one."[1]

Even if Leavis's habitual tantrum of moral signifiers does not quite succeed in creating that functional critical discourse, it seems a world away from the so-called University in Ruins that depresses many today. Leavis remains, in retrospect, a canny diagnostician who anticipates the difficulty and disenchantment we face a half century later. "The advance of science and technology," he writes:

means a human future of change so rapid and of such kinds, of tests and challenges so unprecedented, of decisions and possible non-decisions so momentous and insidious in their consequences, that mankind—this is surely clear—will need to be in full intelligent possession of its full humanity.[2]

I mean to suggest, by passing to a matter of diction, how language often fails the moral thinker, even one most concerned with language. Insofar as Leavis is persuasive, it is because those who read him are steeped in the literature he champions or attacks: without a memorable, and ardently memorized, body of words, without a canon of that kind, one's own words remain abstract counters, a tonic buzz. There must be, to appropriate the title of one of Kermode's books, an "appetite for poetry" that, like manna from heaven, satisfies without satiating, as the church fathers claimed.

---

[1] See especially his essay "Luddites? or, There Is Only One Culture," in *Lectures in America* (New York: Pantheon, 1969), 23.

[2] Ibid., 22.

In Kermode's own creative criticism, the old is renewed by new forms of attention. Consider his interest in the literary relevance of an evolving religious hermeneutics, or his Eliot Lectures on "The Classic" that recall the link between modernization and the revival of learning reaching back to Greece and Rome and even to the Kabbalah.[3] The printing by the humanist editors of carefully vetted ancient texts inspired rather than impeded the emerging national literary vernaculars and helped to spur the Renaissance. It was part of what we would now call a conservative revolution.

Modernism, similarly, was not rejectionist so much as transformative. It sought to defamiliarize, to "make it new" (though Kermode is suitably ironic about the new perpetually replacing the new). Its own conservative revolution maintained something that indeed is a pleasure: the recognition of a continuity made possible by a canon far less monumental than its maligners have claimed, a canon that is able to change, to be changed. "The idea of pleasure," Kermode says forthrightly, "can be positively associated with a changing canonicity." In that respect, pleasure can even be taught, because it is based not on ignorance but on learning.

Change, as we shall see, or change of a nontraumatic kind, is essential to Kermode's argument acknowledging the demise of an older type of literary study yet refusing to see that loss as either just or inevitable. Against the charge of aestheticism, for instance, or of pursuing the *ignis fatuus* of literariness in isolation from social process, he points out that changes in the canon have come from two sources: from the need to refresh perception, to get rid of deadening clichés in politics or art, which led creative writers as well as formalists like Mukařovský to associate the aesthetic function with transgression (especially of so-called bourgeois values), and then from the

---

[3] Kermode, *The Genesis of Secrecy: On the Interpretation of Narrative* (Cambridge, Mass.: Harvard University Press, 1979) and *The Classic: Literary Images of Permanence and Change* (Cambridge, Mass.: Harvard University Press, 1983).

action of time itself, its subversive, disconcerting compound of chance and mutability that makes reinterpretation a necessity.

Kermode sees himself, somewhat sorrowfully, as part of a "remnant." He is caught up in the sense of an ending. At the same time, it is not possible to identify him with this or that school, and he quotes William Empson on the importance of not letting the critic be distracted by any kind of theory, however morally appealing. While theory is necessary to stretch the mind, "however firm your belief in it ... you still have to see whether your feelings can be brought to accept the results" in the particular case.[4]

Empsonian reflections like these put a premium on the individual response, and are less afraid of eccentricity than of conformity. They take their probity and force from being associated with, even soldered to, a notion of close reading or "practical criticism"—"practical" in the sense which I. A. Richards's probe of 1929 put into circulation.[5] Richards methodically investigated the inability of university students (and even some faculty) to interpret unidentified literary passages—that is, to interpret them at sight, unsupported by literary-historical commonplaces. His educationist bent proved essential for both Cambridge English and the New Criticism as they influenced literary studies from the thirties through the late sixties.[6]

One change that has affected criticism since the time of Richards, Leavis, Empson, and Eliot is a closer scrutiny of the language by

[4] Kermode, *An Appetite for Poetry* (Cambridge, Mass.: Harvard University Press, 1989), 45.

[5] *Practical Criticism: A Study of Literary Judgment* (London: Trubner, 1929).

[6] The closeness of moral concern in Richards and Leavis vis-à-vis the changes brought about by the impact of science and technology on their milieux, and the relative slowness with which they felt contemporary education was responding, can be measured by such statements as this from Richards's *Poetry and Science* (1935). Poetry fails us, he writes, if an experienced reader does not change after reading it, if that poetry does not bring about "a permanent alteration of our possibilities as responsive individuals in good or bad adjustment to an all but overwhelming concourse of stimulations." From his reissue of the book as *Poetries and Sciences* (New York: Norton, 1970), 47.

which the literary work is analyzed. There has been a notice-able proliferation of technical terms. The distance between the "rhetoric of criticism," to cite the subtitle of Paul De Man's first collection of essays, *Blindness and Insight* (1971), and the rhetoric of the literature it deals with, points to the fact that, beyond the wish to bring literary study into the human sciences, and to rescue literary appreciation from a chronic impressionism or subjectivism, no metalanguage will now escape suspicion. A backlash charges these linguistic, semiotic, deconstructionist per-petrators with, precisely, a crime against ordinary language, and it deplores their dehumanizing or obfuscating impact on literary education.

I am not jumping into *that* debate. But it should be asked: what general cogency, beyond being a *promesse de bonheur*, a reward for a more complex understanding of tradition or accul-turation, does the criterion of "pleasure" have, revived by Kermode? The question bears on the rhetoric of criticism as well as on the work of art itself. There is clearly more labor than pleasure in reading a highly specialized literary criticism full of borrowed or extended technical terms. "It must give Pleasure," Kermode insists in his own "Notes toward a Supreme Criti-cism." *Pleasure* is a strange word to bear such a strong empha-sis: it is surely on the side of Chaucerian "solas" rather than "sentence." Can it really become as sententious as Kermode wishes it to be?

It all depends on how such a precept, which has its basis in theory as well as experience—if poetics constitutes a theory—works out in practice. Our oldest definition of poetic art holds that the *utile* (or *docere*) and the *dulce* (or *delectare*) should be equally mixed. "Sweetness and Light" is Arnold's extended version. A com-plication is that words, when conscious of the vanity of their mimicry, as in Wallace Stevens, turn into "abysmal instruments" that "make sounds like pips" (not even "like pipes") out of "the sweeping meanings" we impose. How much can be based on

Stevens's cannonade, which so genially deflates a poet's and our bravado as would-be creators?[7]

The word *pleasure* is problematic—I am tempted to say "abysmal"—for several reasons. First, for its onomatopoeic pallor, then for its inability to carry with it the nimbus of its historical associations, lastly—as I will eventually argue—because it glides over the abyss. Though literary elaboration has augmented the vocabulary of feeling and affect, *pleasure* as a critical term remains descriptively poor when thematized this way. Some tribes, anthropologists tell us, have ever so many descriptors for certain natural phenomena, but for us the connotative and semantic field of pleasure is not large. Kermode himself notes that we approach something stronger and more explicitly physical in Wordsworth's celebration of the "grand elementary principle of pleasure," and in contemporary thought through the sexual synonym *jouissance*.

Yet any sexualization of pleasure runs a double danger. The first is the danger of making it appear as if the pleasure linked to art were the by-product of a repression, a successful repression, Freud surmised, but still a sublimated or cerebral derivative, and therefore anything but "disinterested." The second, which Kermode introduces via Roland Barthes's *Le Plaisir du texte*, is that the intense and often transgressive form of pleasure suggested by *jouissance* jeopardizes, like the destructive rather than constructive side of eros, all identity constructs.

---

[7] The figure of the poet, certainly, as distilled from Stevens, is too attractive. The poet is portrayed as fighting a violence from without by a violence from within. Yet the violence in question is in the form of a "war" between mind and sky, between mimetic words and the sheer wonder of the natural world that words seek to render without a false realism or supernaturalism. Stevens's poet pastiches the moon to Virgilian cadences—or cadenzas—especially pastoral and georgic ones, restlessly composing mock-heroic preludes and domestic variations, "petty syllabi, the sounds that stick, inevitably modulating, in the blood." He lives in a place that is not his own, a universe whose blazoned days remind him of man's lack of place even when it produces a "grateful vicissitude" driving the perpetual motor of his verse.

While it is clear that this larger emotion of *jouissance* resembles the "sublime" effect that emanates, according to Edmund Burke and Kant, from objects of reflection that threaten reflection, can literary pleasure really be separated from the merely pleasant once it migrates from art to Blackmur's "discourse of the amateur" or even Barthes's virtuoso conversion of semiotics into a "Lover's discourse"? The rigor of the formalists, their concentration on a work's structure to the exclusion of other features, came about in good part because literary talk had become amateurish—that is, too agreeable. *Plaîre* had already been an imperative in the conversational ethos so important to eighteenth-century French society as it developed parademocratic salons that also advanced the status of women. Often, then, a flirtatious and flattering meaning subsists as an undertone. Cowper's "The Fair commands the Song" is a gallant variant, hinting at subjection rather than freedom, at pleasing the other rather than oneself. Even Kant, characterizing (like Shaftesbury) the beautiful as the source of a "disinterested pleasure," has his difficulty finding a suitable word. The one he chooses, *Wohlgefallen,* bears an involuntary trace of "befell," of an encounter attended by hopeful expectations, as in Spenser's "it chanced" or "it fortuned," which can introduce, of course, a deceptive incident. Borges, with a slyly ominous touch, described "aesthetic reality" as "the imminence of a revelation not yet produced."

None of these definitions, then, quite catches the distinctive enjoyment elicited by art, including the art of reading. Kermode's lament for the critical makers is not only that he gets too little delight from them but also that he cannot feel *their* delight. Where is the inspiring contagion, Hopkins's "the rise, the roll, the carol of creation"? It has not disappeared; it does prevail in other areas, such as the performing arts and especially the response to popular music so close to *jouissance;* indeed, "the arts" now take up an entire separate section of the daily *New York Times.* But in a "society of the spectacle," our own discipline of close, careful, yet imaginative reading cannot find a performative role except by means of this or that outrageous thesis, and so remains, outside the classroom, confined to a thin reception.

If that is so, the pleasure provided by literature or its study must find a new specificity. I respect the challenge Kermode takes up in his concern for canons: the fact that the fate of reading is increasingly tied to the fate of pleasure. For as the exegetical and critical task becomes more specialized, and the public, as Wordsworth foresaw, more dependent on direct, optical or sensory, stimulation, who but an inglorious remnant will appreciate the critic's burden? Even the pleasure of being righteous is harder to come by. The complaint is just, that a need to instrumentalize literature, to convert Stevens's "pips" into "trumpets stern," distorts our focus more than ever, demands that the taint of *otium* be removed from what we do. We therefore seek to apply terms from other disciplines that claim to be closer to social reality, or somehow indispensable.

The basic question that arises is why the change in the study of literature, registered and regretted by Kermode, is uncanonical, that is, not a change on which a renewal of the critical spirit could be based. If the objection is to bad writing, that is hardly a specialty of post-1960s critics: silly comments and judgments are found in any period. It would be easy enough to collect a *sottisier* of Wordsworth criticism, for instance, from 1800 to—well, you name the *terminus ad quem*. Literary study having expanded by democratic leaps and bounds and through a publish-or-perish requirement, it is no wonder that ideological clichés and technical jargon abound. This is not to say that the recession of pleasing prose, or generally of a conversational tone in criticism, does not have its reason. Nor that a redirection of the object of critical attention cannot be justified.

Kermode's *epur si muove* frees up canonicity by showing, like Eliot, a dynamic principle of literary renewal at work, and so removes an antiorthodox prejudice. But it leaves the unfortunate impression that the shift that has indeed occurred, and which Kermode's apt allusion to Chateaubriand's memoirs from beyond the grave depicts as a traumatic discontinuity, is based on a mere, if grievous, misperception. I cannot map out my own understanding of that shift in the time that remains. So I will end with one assertive, overabbreviated thought.

Et in Arcadia ego. The post-Panofskian meaning of that phrase has prevailed. "I too, Death, was in Arcadia." When I suggest that an emphasis on pleasure, however sophisticated, however aware (as Kermode is) of the vacillation of joy and dejection, of delight and dismay—that this emphasis glides over the abyss, I do not mean to deny a principle of utopian hope linked to art's "green thought in a green shade" but wish that emphasis to recognize a shift from the death of Arcady to Arcady as death.

It is a hedonistic politics, a pastoral-utopian "Annihilating all that's made," that prompted Lionel Trilling to surmise, in his essay of 1963 on "The Fate of Pleasure," that "the old connection between literature and politics has been dissolved."[8] I suspect that the literary criticism Kermode is doubtful about has tried—perhaps unsuccessfully—to establish a new connection. Trilling was troubled not only by a redemptive nihilism that has always existed in the form of a religious anticipation or even hastening of the end (that very "sense of an ending" Kermode explored for its fictional resonances in his famous book of that title),[9] but also by something less conscious and willful: the eudaemonic nihilism of a liberal, progressive politics.

Underestimating the permanence of the passions, including religious mania, progressive thought strives to turn the Furies into

---

[8] Collected in Trilling, ed., *Beyond Culture: Essays on Literature and Learning* (New York: Viking, 1965).

[9] Kermode, ed., *The Sense of an Ending: Studies in the Theory of Fiction* (New York: Oxford University Press, 1967).

Eumenides and tames the visionary gleam until it fades into the light of common day. Walter Benjamin had a parallel insight concerning that superliberal nihilism when he defined an impossible choice centering on the reversing relation of modernity and tradition:

The destructive character stands in the front line of the traditionalists. Some pass things down to posterity by making them untouchable and thus conserving them; others pass situations on by making them practicable and thus liquidating them. The latter are called the destructive.[10]

Against the background of the eighteenth-century debate about luxury and the rise of the bourgeoisie, and the contention, in particular, that "the dignity of man was to be found in the principle of pleasure," Trilling sets, starkly, an anticonsumerist force calling itself spiritual, and often in total contempt of pleasure, indeed of worldly society as such. This militant spirituality creates, in the modern period, not only an opposing self but anti-heroes who undermine all social values that used to inspire meliorative political action.

What could be further from Spenser's or Keats's "to enjoy delight with liberty" than Dostoyevski's Underground Man? "To know and feel and live and move at the behest of the principle of pleasure—this, for the Underground Man," Trilling writes, "so far from constituting his native and naked dignity, constitutes his humiliation in bondage."

Trilling does not view such devaluation of pleasure as "merely an event of a particular moment of culture." Freud's *Beyond the Pleasure Principle* shows it to be a permanent fact of the psychic life. Yet Trilling reprehends the blindness of contemporary thinkers who fail to see that unpleasure too demands to be satisfied—by

---

[10] *Reflections: Essays, Aphorisms, Autobiographical Writings*, translated by Edmund Jephcott, edited by Peter Demetz (New York: Harcourt Brace, 1978), 301–3.

a "gratification...not within the purview of ordinary democratic progressivism."

Modern art's "experiment in the negative transcendence of the human" (Trilling's words) is no longer an experiment today. What will repair the breach between a moral politics and the brutalism of much contemporary art—as well as of the realities of daily life—when terror strikes and the scars of the spirit are clearly visible? In "Resolution and Independence," Wordsworth's asceticism, his minimalist plot and nonopulence of diction (sensitively noted by Kermode), manage to draw an image of life rather than death from a solitary old man harvesting leeches from a pool "bare to the eye of heaven." But these Wordsworthian qualities also remind us of something ghostly and elementary linked to poverty and unpleasure. As if he were an apparition, the leech gatherer comes upon the poet "unawares," absorbed by "fears and fancies," "dim sadness," and nameless "blind thoughts." If these are thoughts about blindness, about wishing to become blind to the world, not just unclear inner sentiments, if they are repressed and tempting apocalyptic fantasies in the very poet whose program it is to humanize imagination, to link imagination more firmly to "this goodly universe," then nihilism enters here into the very heart of benevolence and its visionary quest. This depiction of the leech gatherer interprets the man's force of spirituality, what Wordsworth calls, using the plainest words, a "leading from above." The old man in his rocklike aspect is a simple, realistic figure as denuded as the desolate moor; there is nothing supernatural about him. He is the opposite of a transcendent guide. Yet he is nevertheless a border image tempting the poet to view him as a ghostly image, an admonitory, spectral visitant. An uncanny feeling, abetted by the idea of a covert, preternatural source of vitality, is in danger of taking over.

Wordsworth always scrupulously notes what arouses, and sometimes baffles, his imagination. The powerlessness of this grave liver, who seems scarcely alive, has to become a source of power for the poet, a peculiar sort of inspiration.[11] Social sympathy need not be ruled out as a motive for this charged instant. But another—by no means contrary—impulse is poetry's competitiveness with divinity through Wordsworth's refusal to forgo the intensity of secular perception.

The poem, I venture to conclude, is about a reversal of powerlessness into power of spirit, rather than about an alternation of despondency and joy which can, of course, accompany that reversal. (In the *Prelude*, when Wordsworth describes his response to the tumult of the French Revolution, including the Terror, he admits to "daring sympathies with Power.") Unpower/power, not the pleasure/unpleasure complex, is the problematic subject, as it is also in contemporary moral philosophers like Emmanuel Levinas and Maurice Blanchot. Kermode's meditation on loss, on the passing in his lifetime of the idea of a literary canon that pleased many generations yet was open to change—in short, a canon empowering rather than imposing—runs parallel to his understanding of "Resolution and Independence." Yet it skirts the political impasse that presently makes literary criticism, not only literature, a troubled mirror of our culture.

[11] Kermode points to Wordsworth's dilemma when he writes: "The stony steadfastness of the old man...is quite another matter from the excited action of the poetic spirit, and the contrast hints at the pain of the more secular form of election."

It Must Be Abstract

JOHN GUILLORY

I would like first to thank the Tanner Committee for inviting me to give a response to Professor Kermode's lectures and Professor Kermode himself for provoking me in his subtle remarks to think once more—yet once more—about the literary canon, "tedious and battered" subject though it is, as he remarks in his first lecture. It has been especially challenging to formulate my responses to these lectures, not only because I share a fairly large area of agreement with Professor Kermode about the matters I think we both consider to be most deeply important, but also because his lectures belong to a body of work which will, I believe, continue to be of great interest to scholars of the future, when so much criticism, both past and present, is undeniably and deservedly perishable.

Let me begin, then, by noting briefly the area of my agreement with Professor Kermode, before suggesting some of the ways in which I would depart from the terms of his analysis. I do agree that literary criticism is a curiously troubled discipline today, and that part of its trouble is directly related to the ambivalence that academic literary critics seem to express toward the object of their discipline. This ambivalence typically takes two forms: first, the disinclination to regard works of literature as the necessary or con-stitutive object of literary criticism, and second, an even stronger aversion to a way of talking about literature in which the pleasure of the literary work is acknowledged as its chief reason for being, and correlatively that the communication of that pleasure to the readers of criticism is at least one of the purposes of criticism. There is, in my view, and I take it in Professor Kermode's as well, something symptomatic of dysfunction in the pervasive embarrassment with the subject of pleasure, and the ease with which pleasure has been neutralized as the merely contingent effect of reception—subject, in other words, to the irremediably relativizing effect of historical change.

It is something of a relief, however, that Professor Kermode does not give us the usual exercise in revanchist rhetoric, but an impressively measured reflection on the fate of pleasure in literary work from the perspective of his long career. In a moment, I would like to suggest that the tone of his lectures participates integrally in the argument he has to make about pleasure, since he conceives aesthetic pleasure in its highest form as necessarily intermingled with the prospect or experience of loss. But of that in a moment. Here, at the outset of my remarks, I would like to remind us of certain continuities which have persisted across Professor Kermode's two dispensations, or terrestrial globes, the latter of which has presumably seen the demise of the literary object as it was formerly defined, as the object which always gives pleasure, while always changing.

This latter dispensation is defined, to be sure, by a turn toward historical, social, and above all political concerns. But Professor Kermode only glances at the general character of this dispensation, without resorting to naming names or denouncing positions. The effect is at once to confer a greater seriousness upon his argument, but also perhaps to underestimate how much continuity there is in the history of criticism. The turn to the political is one way critics have of doing what they have always done, which is to neutralize pleasure on behalf of more socially acceptable—or as the case may be, more socially transgressive—agendas. This tendency of criticism was remarked very shrewdly by Joseph Schumpeter long ago in 1942, long before our recent political turn, and from the vantage of his discipline—political economy—which was then competing ever more successfully with literary criticism for dominance of the public sphere. Schumpeter traces the origins of the adversarial or politicized intellectual to the humanist scholar of the sixteenth century: "The humanists were primarily philologists but...they quickly expanded into the fields of manners, politics, religion and philosophy. This was not alone due to the contents of the classic works which they interpreted along with their grammar—from the criticism of a text to the criticism of a society, the way is shorter than it seems."[1] Thomas More might be taken as the great model for the first of the politicized critics, and the way was short indeed for him from philology to social criticism, and short to the executioner's block as well.

Schumpeter in fact was only too happy to dismiss the literarily trained critic of society as simply obsolete, permanently displaced by the economist, the political scientist, the sociologist, but literary critics have never consented to be dismissed so readily. During the period spanning the century from Carlyle to Eliot, Richards, and Leavis, and then again since the 1980s, a host of literary critics have found the short way to social criticism, what was once called *Kulturkritik* and what I would call authoritarian cultural criticism. By "authoritarian" I mean that critics of the nineteenth century based their critiques of society on the authority of culture and its study, which at that time was still capable of competing successfully in the public sphere with those experts who studied the realms of politics or the economy. Our new cultural critics are very much in this line, although their prestige in the public sphere has diminished. They share with their predecessors the same problematic tendency to neutralize the pleasure of the literary work on behalf of what would once have been regarded as moral uplift, and would perhaps now be regarded as a progressive politics. In either case, the encounter with a cultural work becomes an occasion for confirming or contesting the belief systems expressed in the work.

---

[1] Joseph A. Schumpeter, *Capitalism, Socialism, and Democracy* (New York: Harper and Row, 1942), 148.

This long-standing tendency of criticism toward a certain moralism or puritanism, even sometimes paradoxically in the case of those critics who extol an ethic of transgressive pleasure, puts a certain pressure on the process of canonical selection, which it may not be possible to resist. That is to say, canon formation has always proceeded with an entirely inadequate account of evaluation, one which in the end usually invokes what Professor Kermode calls, following Gadamer, "prejudices." The most interesting critics since Kant have wrestled with just this problem, and sometimes attempted to resolve it by isolating the experience of aesthetic pleasure and extolling it in the work of art as a "higher pleasure," distinct either in kind or degree from the pleasures rendered by other human experiences. I am myself on record as affirming the specificity of aesthetic pleasure—its difference from other kinds of pleasures—but I would like to argue here for a position which I believe departs from Professor Kermode's, in not claiming for this pleasure a higher status, and therefore not claiming for the domain of culture the higher authority upon which cultural criticism was and continues to be based.

The most singular and unmistakable symptom of authoritarian cultural criticism was until recently the reduction of literature to the instance of poetry. This reduction is very much present in the claims Matthew Arnold makes for poetry, and recurs in the even greater claims made by I. A. Richards for a conception of the poetic art as that which orders or organizes all human affects. Only poetry, said Richards famously.

It is a rather spectacular irony of the most recent versions of cultural criticism that claims of this sort are no longer routed through poetry. But these two facts are in my view causally connected. The inflated claims made for poetry are directly related to the decline of poetry as a vital art form in the modern world (at least in the West), at present now a very minor subculture in a vast domain of cultural production.

One way to understand recent criticism's retreat from poetry is as a strategic regrounding of the authoritarian claims of cultural criticism in the domain of mass culture. This strategy has given us cultural studies, trouble with a capital *T* for the literary canon. My point is that cultural studies is very much in the direct line of Carlyle, Arnold, Eliot, and Richards in claiming that the domain of culture is the most appropriate ground upon which to erect a criticism of society as a whole. This strategy has been a mistake, not so much because it has moved criticism away from literature, but because it has simply transferred to another domain of culture the claims historically made for the work of art, and for the critic.

The inflation of the claims made for art has recently been subjected to a searching and persuasive critique by Jean-Marie Schaeffer in his book *Art of the Modern Age,* and in lieu of rehearsing his argument at any length, I would simply like to appropriate the main point he makes, that the fortunes of the aesthetic, and of aesthetic pleasure, have been made to rest too entirely on the certified forms of high art—poetry, painting, sculpture, music, architecture.[2] It was as a result of this philosophical overburdening of high art that aesthetic pleasure became so vulnerable to moralistic or political neutralization. The effect of monumentalization to which Professor Kermode draws our attention in quoting from Stevens's "Notes toward a Supreme Fiction"—itself an example, however beautiful, of this philosophical overburdening of art—can be understood immediately in this context. The monumentalized work of art overshoots the effect of pleasure altogether and makes a demand upon the recipient for a reverent response, regardless of whether pleasure is experienced or not. A monument makes a demand without answering a need.

Works of art would surely be enjoyed and evaluated less anxiously if the specificity of aesthetic pleasure generally were decoupled from the status of the high-art work. The great problem of the

---

[2] Jean-Marie Schaeffer, *Art of the Modern Age: Philosophy of Art from Kant to Heidegger,* translated by Steven Randall (Princeton, N.J.: Princeton University Press, 2000).

high arts in the twentieth century has proven again and again to
be the expansion of the aesthetic domain of culture, the copresence
of myriad works of mass culture along with works of high art,
so-called. Without opening this door too widely, I would like to
endorse Schaeffer's conclusion that aesthetic pleasure must be
conceived not so much as a higher pleasure but as a specific kind of
pleasure, one of many kinds of pleasure. The reduction of art
to the instance of poetry, which was the symptom of its overburdening, might be countered by an emphasis on *poiesis*, human
making in general, as it pervades so much of our everyday lives.
The restriction of aesthetic pleasure to the certified work of art has
been a consequential philosophical error, even if many great works
of art have assumed just this error.

In any case, I believe it is far too late historically to claim for
the works of high art effects either of religious transcendence—
salvational effects—which few would venture to advocate openly
though many advocate tacitly, or of philosophical profundity,
the work of art as an embodiment of truths that can be expressed
in philosophical terms. The aesthetic domain is on the contrary
ubiquitous—or should be. Our speech, our manners, our bearing,
our dress, our houses, our furnishings, our public spaces and
private entertainments should all be beautiful, should deliver their
measure of aesthetic pleasure. The failure of this view of aesthetic
pleasure to achieve anything like consensus was perfectly obvious
most recently in the huffy response of Jonathan Franzen to the
embrace of Oprah Winfrey, who did not understand, it would
seem, that Franzen's novel belonged "solidly," as he declared in
an interview, "in the high art tradition." That is to say, it was
intended to deliver the kind of aesthetic pleasure that *distinguished* it from the pleasures of other similar-seeming sorts of
objects—objects which only looked like novels or poems or plays,
but which were not really art at all, because the quality of their
pleasure was not complex enough. Only a certain kind of pleasure,
on this view, entitles a work to the epithet *aesthetic* and therefore,

presumably, entitles a work to enter, briefly or permanently, the company of the high arts.

This brings me to two final points I should like to make about the argument of Professor Kermode's lectures—and here I must contend more openly, if also as cautiously as I can, with the notion of aesthetic pleasure that he recommends to us.

This notion is distinguished by its mixing of pain and pleasure; the latter Professor Kermode calls, most interestingly, "dismay." Is there indeed a particular kind of aesthetic pleasure, higher than sherry and rope dancing, to be found in certain works, which qualifies them as true works of art, that is, eligible for canonicity? I would like to get at this question very crudely by remarking my own puzzlement at the allusion to Stevens's "Notes toward a Supreme Fiction" in our two lectures. One hopes there might be a third lecture forthcoming someday, corresponding to the missing section of Stevens's poem "It Must Be Abstract." (This would be the third lecture, because Professor Kermode reverses the order of Stevens's three sections, from abstraction, change, pleasure to the reverse.) Abstraction, as a quality of the supreme fiction, which is itself a kind of philosophical term for the cultural project of poetry, is missing from Professor Kermode's lectures, except perhaps implicitly as a possible analogue for the negation of pleasure which is at once the bad agenda of our latter-day politicized or cultural critics, whose response to literature seems so arid and academic, but also *present* as perhaps another name for the experience of loss or the possibility of loss which is imputed to the specifically higher pleasure of the canonical work of art. Remember that Stevens associates the injunction to be abstract with the death of the gods—"the death of one god is the death of all"—and with the loss not just of Eden but of the explanatory power of the myth of the Fall.

There are two problems here which might be sorted out by means of the missing term, *abstraction.*

First, there is the problem of the relation between the kind of pleasure that belongs specifically to the experience of the artwork or the poem, and the equally particular pleasure that belongs to the work that literary critics do in research and writing about literature. These are not the same experiences exactly, but one is presumably the ground of the other. In the case of academic criticism, it may be that the pleasure of research or argument sometimes takes off, as it were, from the ground of the experience of the literary work. When that happens, it becomes possible to forget the being of the literary work as aesthetic, and thus to reduce it to the mere occasion of other kinds of pleasure, or to the neutralization of pleasure altogether. This, I would admit, is a general tendency of academic criticism today. The notion that literary works can be understood as transparently revealing social or historical reality is the unfortunate effect of this tendency, against which Professor Kermode protests. This is a problem which can only by addressed by renewed attention to the formal properties of literary works as aesthetic works, which means taking account both experientially and theoretically of their aims, including the aim of giving pleasure. The general principle here is that it is a mistake in approaching an object of study not to acknowledge what kind of object it is. Biologists take pleasure in studying germs, but it is not an aim of germs to give pleasure, nor do biologists enjoy having the flu.

The remedy Professor Kermode proposes, however, for redirecting our attention to the specificity of the aesthetic leaves temporarily behind his own considerable work on literary form and offers an interesting and (to me) puzzling return to the notion of the touchstone, derived of course from Arnold's 1860 essay, "The Study of Poetry." It is clear enough that what Professor Kermode wants is a model for the initial experience of pleasure in the literary work and, at the same time, an explanation for why this experience can be considered a "higher pleasure," that is, ultimately a justification for canonical status. Quite carefully he asserts that it isn't so much that the same works always produce the same aesthetic effect, but that whatever works are at any moment canonical can be said to produce this effect. Hence the canon accommodates change while always providing us with a specific higher pleasure.

Surely the most interesting conjecture to emerge from these fertile meditations is that it might be possible to give a psychological account, as it were, of the touchstone experience. Yet I would like to suggest that this psychology is underdeveloped in Professor Kermode's argument, because the hypothesis of a pleasure which is intermixed with loss and dismay is contaminated by the narrative of the decline of literary criticism, a narrative that constitutes the framing assumption of the lectures. It is easy to see that what is potentially lost or at stake in the examples from Wordsworth, Eliot, and Dante is literature itself, poetry itself. The loss that shadows the aesthetic experience is the loss that currently threatens the profession of literary study, the loss of its object. This dread accounts for the fact that the touchstones end up having a surprisingly similar meaning, regardless of their source.

This homogeneity is particularly troubling in the case of Professor Kermode's citation of Eliot's touchstones, which powerfully analogize sexual and aesthetic pleasure. This analogy gains its power by imputing to sexual experience a complexity that also, in a way, diminishes the range of joys sexuality is capable of bringing us in the real world. Eliot's touchstones implicitly identify the complex pleasure of the work of art with the complexity inhering for him in the experience of sexual surrender, the notion that sexual experience was all the more noble because it was fallen and evil and damning. But against Eliot, I would quote William Empson, who saw through the psychology of the Eliotic touchstone in his tart comment on Eliot's revulsion at Milton's representation of unfallen sexual pleasure in *Paradise Lost*: "So long as you gave Mr. Eliot images of someone being tortured his nerves were at peace, but if you gave him an image of two people making each other happy he screamed."[3] My point in quoting Empson is not to dismiss the notion of the touchstone altogether, but to draw attention to a curious contradiction within it. Eliot's touchstones are in fact highly idiosyncratic, precisely because they express his very personal, individual relation to sexuality. His touchstones are little idiosyncratic canons, exactly what canons are not supposed to be. Just by striving to be canonical exemplars, they collapse back into the utterly idiosyncratic, even into the expression of an individual pathology. This little exercise in reading the touchstones, which really only builds on what Professor Kermode has already observed in these lectures, is intended to remind us of how difficult it is to generalize any principle from the experience of aesthetic pleasure that would ground a principle of evaluation or canonicity. We are simply a long way from being able to do this.

My response to this uncertainty would be to retreat from attempting to make the connection between the quality of pleasure and the judgment of canonicity, and further to withdraw the claim that aesthetic pleasures are in any defensible sense "higher pleasures." The tendency to argue for the higher pleasures of the aesthetic is just what sets us down the road toward the inflation of the work of art. The inflated claims for the great work of art, the canonical work, usually come at the expense of the aesthetic dimension itself, in its myriad forms, not just high art, not just poetry. The same error accounts for the derogation of supposedly simpler human pleasures, on behalf of propping up the work of art against any competing pleasure.

If the pleasures and pains of sexuality are more varied for some of us, I hope most of us, than Eliot's experience of this human affect, so might be the pleasures and pains of the aesthetic. Complex pleasures may be mixtures of pleasure and pain, but complex pleasures are only preferable to simple ones when it is complex

---

[3] William Empson, *Milton's God* (Cambridge: Cambridge University Press, 1961), 30.

pleasures that we seek. I believe that the greatest art gives us very complex pleasures indeed, but I don't think that such pleasure must come at the expense of other kinds of pleasure, or require their derogation as merely simple. It may seem right to think that aesthetic pleasures are the highest kind, but the most I am willing to claim is that human existence would be sadly incomplete without aesthetic pleasure. This pleasure is no more nor less necessary to our humanness than the pleasures of sex, food, conversation, and many others. I would argue, then, for the diversity of human pleasures rather than their hierarchization; and I would like to believe that the greatest works of the human spirit can be better preserved by preserving a lively sense of the range of human pleasures, both simple and complex. It is only by such generosity, which is otherwise everywhere to be found in the work of Frank Kermode, that works of art will escape the annulment of their pleasures, the effect of monumentalization that is always the risk of their elevation to the status of canonicity.

The Artist and the Canon

CAREY PERLOFF

It's a great pleasure to be part of this illustrious group, although I am here as a total outsider, having no claims to academic expertise on the subject of the canon. However, as a theater artist and as artistic director of a large American theater, because I wrestle with questions of the canon on a daily basis as I decide how to program the work that we do, I find these questions of the nature of canonicity fascinating. In today's eloquent lecture on change, Kermode asserts that the canon is constantly in the process of change, but while he gives persuasive examples of work that has disappeared from and then reentered the canon in felicitous ways, he offers no real explanation as to why this should be the case. "There is no intrinsic preservative, but somebody at some point must have thought these were good things, and so began the history of their success."

Who is this somebody? Kermode asserts that "this person need not be a professional scholar," but I believe he overlooks in a crucial way who that person is most likely to be. In my view, canons are not formed by "theological fiat or pedagogical fiat ... or chance," nor, despite the significant contributions of the many brilliant critics in this room and elsewhere, by literary critics, but by the artists themselves. In almost every case in which there is a marked shift in the canon, or a renewed interest in so-called noncanonical writers or composers or visual artists, the impetus has come from particular artists who bring certain works back into focus through their own creative reaction to, or influence by, those works. While life may inspire the content of art to some degree, I firmly believe that the form art takes grows out of an artist's rigorous encounter with other works of art. This is why, again *pace* the critics in the room, artists and writers are usually the most interesting critics. Kermode speaks persuasively about how Eliot "elevated Middleton and Tourneur to modernity, an essential step toward their preservation." Clearly, Eliot's critical tastes were guided by his own aesthetic imperatives, which is why they are so interesting and so unusual. For example, at a time when the classical canon virtually ignored the fascinating prose narratives of the first and second centuries AD, Eliot rescued one of the greatest, *The Satiricon*, by weaving it in very subtle ways into *The Waste Land*. One of the central images of *The Waste Land* is that of the Sybil of Cumae, who hangs in her cage and, when asked what she wants, answers, "I want to die." That touchstone phrase, and the imagery of death by water which pervades *The Waste Land* and owes strong derivation to *The Satiricon*, helped make Petronius matter again. Suddenly, the qualities that classical philologists had abhorred about *The Satiricon*, like the fractured narrative, shifting point of view, ironic juxtaposition, and jargon and slang sharing space with elevated language, were celebrated as they were seen through the modernist lens provided by poets such as Eliot. Of course, the Petronius that we read and adore today is quite a different writer from the one Romans encountered in the first century, because his work has come to us in the fractured form so beloved of modernist poets. But Eliot himself would have been the first to acknowledge the reciprocal change that happens to a work from the past as it encounters our present prejudices.

To take one of Professor Kermode's own examples, in the past decade, baroque composers such as Handel and Monteverdi (and their sister playwrights Marivaux and Musset) have made a reappearance in the canon. I would join Kermode in saluting this felicitous return, but again I would argue that it is not because Handel's work has "fallen into the hands of understanding editors" that Handel has returned. On the contrary. Mostly Mozart always sells, as does anything by Verdi and Puccini. The baroque rarely does. Why then is it being programmed everywhere today? Because artists are demanding it. In the 1990s, important stage directors like Mark Lamos, Peter Sellars, and Stephen Wadsworth began finding enormous contemporary muscle in baroque music, and making a persuasive case for it on stage. And how did their attention get turned to this music? Often by composers and singers themselves. Steve Reich, one of the most important composers in America today, has sought to find a vocal language in direct contradiction to what he perceives as the vocal mannerisms of the bel canto tradition. In seeking vigorous vocal music that is rhythmically vivid, proudly declarative, and not tied to Mozartean harmonies, he has naturally sought out operas like *Rinaldo* or *The Coronation of Poppea* and singers like Cheryl Bensman-Rowe and Lorraine Hunt, to fuel his own vocal triumphs like *Tehillim*. Artists call upon other artists to make their cases, to rebel against the current norm, to find new forms. And as they do, the canon shifts.

This is why I think we should stop bemoaning the fact that some canonical authors or artists have fallen by the wayside in the supposedly philistine culture we inhabit. What is critical is that every artist's touchstones are likely to be different. When a body of literature no longer serves as a touchstone for creative work, it will fade temporarily from the radar screen. This is not the end of the world; if the given work has the muscle to awaken future generations, it will come back into vogue at a later date. If Romantic poetry, for example, with its exquisite meditations on pleasure and pain, does not seem to be central to the current interests of American undergraduates or the reading public today, perhaps it is because it is not providing valuable fodder for those writers or artists who are most exciting in the culture today. We had a vigorous debate at yesterday's lecture about the meaning of the word *pleasure,* and about the relationship of pleasure to power, a subject to which I hope we can return at greater length in the seminar tomorrow. Since no formal definitions were offered of exactly how the term *pleasure* was being used, I would venture to offer my own. I believe pleasure in relation to a work of art is directly proportional to the creative activity it awakens in the viewer or the reader. Perhaps this is close to Victor Shklovsky's definition of great art as that which defamiliarizes our own world such that we see it anew. This pleasure of awakening is muscular, and when it occurs in the mind of a creative artist, new creative output ensues. The great video artist Bill Viola's sensual pleasure in the mysterious figures in a Mantegna altar piece triggered a major piece of video art (now displayed at the National Gallery in London) that reanimates Mantegna while illuminating Viola's own aesthetic.

Harold Pinter's encounter with the very early work of Beckett in 1954 triggered such an extreme form of what I would call "pleasure" that it launched a writing career in direct response to that encounter. "The more he grinds my nose in the shit the more I am grateful to him," Pinter wrote in 1954.[1] This is surely a different kind of pleasure from that afforded by reading Wordsworth, but it is a fertile and creative pleasure. "I'll buy his goods hook, line and sinker, because he leaves no stone unturned and no maggot lonely. He brings forth a body of beauty." It was not literary critics (and, God knows, not drama critics!) who helped coax Beckett into the canon. It was writers like Pinter, who recognized Beckett's genius long before the critical establishment did so, and insisted that it be taken seriously. In this country, David Mamet has done for Pinter very much what Pinter did for Beckett. Another example: suddenly, after many years, the poet A. E. Housman is being read and discussed today, not just in academe but by, yes, those general readers we seem to believe have all but disappeared. Why? Because Tom Stoppard wrote a play about him, *The Invention of Love*, which stimulated a major reevaluation of Housman's

[1] *Various Voices* (New York: Grove Press, 1998), 55.

work and his place in literary history. Suddenly Housman had muscle again; his work stimulated other creative work, and therefore it returned to the canon.

To segue here to another point, it was also Stoppard who, in his play *Travesties*, reignited interest in those most vigorously uncanonical authors, the Dadaists. In this regard, it is disappointing to me that when we discuss the canon of English literature, we take the myopic view that because works are written in English they have more business being grouped together than, let us say, works from various cultures that share a formal or spiritual impetus. In the visual arts, such a literal nationalist grouping would be considered impossible: one cannot talk about the Italian futurist painter Marinetti without also examining the Russian futurist painter Malevich; we talk about the music of Arvo Paart and that of Steve Reich in one breath, although the former is Czech and the latter American.

Clearly, literature is bounded by language in a way that music and the visual arts are not. But again, I would argue that the habit in American and British universities of grouping literatures solely by national boundaries flies in the face of how much of the best writing happens. I am currently working on a new production of Schiller's *Don Carlos* for the American Conservatory Theater, and there is nary a scene in that play that doesn't have a direct allusion to *Hamlet*. But then the same is true of Pirandello's *Enrico IV*, which I directed at A.C.T. last season. Schiller's encounter with Shakespeare changed the face of his writing and brought Shakespeare so deeply into the German consciousness that many Germans still believe Shakespeare was really written in German. Artists have always been interested in work across linguistic borders: one can't understand Pinter without understanding his love for Kafka, and on and on. In fact, I would hold that artists have been much more intrepid than critics in seeking out international literatures to bring into the canon. And surely that is a part of canonical change which we should embrace.

Finally, since Professor Hartman spoke yesterday about Arcadia, about Arcadia not only as a locus for pleasure but for "unpleasure," for death, for pain, and because there seems to be such general despondency about the interest of the general reader in the Arcadian truths so dear to lovers of literature, I returned last night to a favorite speech of mine from Stoppard's play *Arcadia*, which wrestles with this very question of canonicity, of change, of what remains in the canon and what is jettisoned. The brilliant young mathematician Thomasina is in despair and says to her tutor, Septimus: "Oh Septimus, can you bear it? All the lost plays of the Athenians! Two hundred at least by Aeschylus, Sophocles, Euripides—thousands of poems—Aristotle's own library brought to Egypt by Cleopatra's ancestors! How can we sleep for grief?" And Septimus replies:

By counting our stock. Seven plays from Aeschylus, seven from Sophocles, nineteen from Euripides, my lady! You should no more grieve for the rest than for a buckle lost from your first shoe, or for your lesson book which will be lost when you are old. We shed as we pick up, like travelers who must carry everything in their arms, and what we let fall will be picked up by those behind. The procession is very long and life is very short. We die on the march. But there is nothing outside the march so nothing can be lost to it. The missing plays of Sophocles will turn up, piece by piece, or be written again in another language.[2]

And thus the canon continues to evolve.

[2] Tom Stoppard, *Arcadia* (London: Faber and Faber, 1993), 38.

Reply to Commentators

FRANK KERMODE

On the Comments of the Discussants

I'm grateful to Professors Guillory and Hartman for their patience and Professor Perloff's general comments—the lectures they had to comment on were rather remote from the subject they had been led to expect—and for the courtesy of their responses. Guillory even gave his remarks the title I should have used if there had been provision for a third lecture, though I did not plan to use it quite as he did. I chose an old and weary theme and was relieved that he could approve of the way I didn't treat it—as "the usual exercise in revanchist rhetoric." I take it that the time has long passed for protest against all that has happened in our field of study. If it hadn't done so by the time of the lectures, it almost certainly has done so by now. My present answer to the question how to be a critic is one I borrowed long ago from William Empson: take what theoretical help you fancy, but follow your nose, and I am glad to see it quoted in one of its forms by Professor Hartman. Not everybody has a nose in this sense—there is an enological analogy—and in either case, if you don't have one, you should seek some other form of employment. Of course a great many people do that, and it is no disgrace.

If it should chance that literature as such means very little to you, having no nose you can trust, nothing you say on the subject will have a value appropriate to comment on that subject. You may say many things about other topics that some work of literature happens to present to your mind, but their value would pertain to another subject and have little to do with a topic your activities suggest you know and care very little about. Call that topic "poetry" and ask whether you have any in your head—any that is truly part of your mind. If not, keep on doing something else instead.

I seem to have caused real pain by mentioning touchstones, but although I dwelt a moment on Arnold's touchstones, I tried to make it plain that I didn't like them, or his motive for having them. What I had in mind and didn't, perhaps, explain very well, was precisely those works, or even those lines, that give pleasure, and part of the point was that they are not fixed. It is simply against common sense that mine will be identical with yours, or with Arnold's, or with those of any future readers who live in a different world and have in their heads a body of work that cannot closely resemble mine, if only because there have been more good poems, or whatever, in the interim. This being inescapably so, it seemed reasonable to allude to Arnold's choices in this connection of pleasure and change. But the shock of finding Arnold mentioned at all appears to have precluded consideration of this point.

I have pondered Mr. Guillory's point that critics have always neutralized pleasure, quite strongly wishing it to be untrue, though I am prepared to believe that a great many of them, past and present, do mistrust or don't know pleasure in this context and turn away from its source as soon as possible. One simple reason for this is that almost anything is easier to do, and easier to teach, than genuine criticism. I don't think Schumpeter is a great help at this point; it isn't what the humanists did. Settling *hoti*'s business is perfectly proper and needs to be done if you are reviving the Greek language, but it is not, in the more usual sense of the word, literary criticism. Schumpeter was referring to humanists, *hoti*-definers. And of course he was right to say that many of them took to politics and theology, but that is barely relevant to the present case, since they were not, in the sense we have been using, critics.

As it happens, I long ago wrote about the terrific problem *hoti* creates in the interpretation of Mark 4:12, actually by not being there, having been unexpectedly replaced by *hina*, which reverses the sense. The grammarian must decide whether Mark (whose Greek may have been shaky, but these are very common words) was using *hina* wrongly, or in an unusual way, or defend the extremely unwelcome idea that Jesus told parables to deceive the people and cheat them of salvation. So the humanists have a crucial philological task, and, in the light of their decisions, the theologians have a theological one. Even critics, I admit, must sometimes call on knowledge of more than a single line to settle such arguments: were Dorothy Wordsworth's eyes "wild" or "mild"? I believe this turns on a manuscript reading and is a job for a scholar, though he might not be too strict to introduce other evidence about the character of Dorothy. Just so, the decision between *hoti* and *hina* is a strictly philological one, yet one can see how repugnant some have found *hina* on nonphilological grounds and why they sought philological grounds for emending it.

Neutralizing pleasure is a task that may be carried out in various ways, but it seems odd to regard it as a good thing. And it is wrong, as I argued in the lectures, to treat transgression as necessarily the enemy of pleasure, thus linking it, in Guillory's mind, with using "a cultural work" as "an occasion for confirming or contesting the belief systems expressed in the work."

Guillory's fear of pleasure is clearly expressed in his views on the canon. He accuses others of a kind of puritanism, and attacks the notion that some things give more pleasure than others, holding that it is unfair to claim privilege for the "higher," since what is normally thought to deserve that label can be regarded as a "very minor subculture in a vast domain of cultural production." It seems clear from his discussion of Jean-Marie Schaeffer's book that he himself is repelled by works of art that have elicited responses of which he disapproves—a "reverent response," for instance. Anything that elicits such a response "makes a demand without answering a need"—not a need felt by Guillory, that is. If I feel strongly about any part of his argument, it is his assumption that it is possible and desirable to adjust the "height of response," to decouple aesthetic pleasure from "high" art, and to decide whether somebody else's response is "far too late historically." This view makes him an enemy of Jonathan Franzen, but this is surely only a matter of terminology, the offensive use of "high." I cannot believe Professor Guillory does not have experience of the difference between serious fiction and rubbish. It is a fact of life, however difficult it may be to philosophize it.

I will add only a word about the account of what is at stake in the examples I gave about the part of loss in pleasure (it might have been obliging of me, and quite easy, to have illustrated the point with a selection of pop songs). It is said that the loss that shadows the aesthetic experience is the loss of the object of literary study. This is ingenious but irrelevant, like the claim that aesthetic pleasure may be had in equal measure from sex, food, conversation. This is a misunderstanding (despite the bonus of a certain limited democratic satisfaction) that belongs to a party to which I cannot belong. I have nothing against conversation, sex, or food. But I think I know the difference between them and a great poem. I say this not merely out of a conviction (felt along the pulses) that I am right, but because I genuinely regret that people who seem perfectly qualified to agree prefer to say—are, it seems, unable to say otherwise—that they have wholly comparable experiences from a television soap and Dante.

These disconnected remarks have arisen from musings over Guillory's essay. In the course of it, some differences of opinion arose in respect of Wallace Stevens, a poet whom I greatly admire. It occurs to me as I end these observations that there is a passage in which Stevens offers perhaps as good an idea of a pleasure in poetry associated with something like dismay, almost of fear. It occurs in the unusually protracted meditation of his "Canon Aspirin." Here is part of it:

...To discover an order as of
A season, to discover summer and know it,

To discover winter and know it well, to find,
Not to impose, not to have reasoned at all,
Out of nothing to have come on major weather,

It is possible, possible, possible. It must
Be possible. It must be that in time
The real will from its crude compoundings come,

Seeming, at first, a beast disgorged, unlike,
Warmed by a desperate milk....

Geoffrey Hartman is a scholar whose learned criticism long ago won him the respect of his contemporaries, and his work in other fields has done much to enhance that respect. And I am gratefully aware that he has always given to my work any respect it deserves, but I do not think it can be enhanced by collocating it with the failures, or even with the successes, of F. R. Leavis. My failures are not at all of the same sort, nor are my successes, if I have any, which Leavis would have been happy to deny. Nor, when I used an expression of Valéry's, did I have it in mind (any more than Valéry did) to recommend a patristic analogy between poetry and manna. I rejoin Hartman only when he cites that remark of Empson's. And Empson, who took very deep pleasure in poetry, would not have scorned the idea that in doing so he won a promise of happiness. (Incidentally, he was also knowledgeable about dismay.) Like Mr. Guillory, like the legendary Oxford don I cited, Hartman is very uneasy about pleasure. He fears for its health, detecting in its countenance a hint of an "onomatopoeic pallor," a symptom I find too obscure to interpret, though it finally emerges that the illness of pleasure arises from its sexualization, and its consequent association with transgressiveness.

What he says here about this limitation is certainly of interest, and the introduction of the sublime into the discussion was timely. But he is clear that pleasure, in the end, is something not to be expected from professorial discourse, even when that discourse is "our own discipline of close, careful, yet imaginative reading." I'm not sure I know who are the "we" behind that "our," only that it seems reasonable to ask that they be enabled to "feel their delight" since there surely ought to be some in imaginative reading. Unless I have completely misunderstood the sense of "our," Hartman of course must be one of the group, but his point here seems to be that it is a qualification for membership to write clumsily, that it is somehow wrong to deplore bad writing, which must be defended as a necessary consequence of specialization. Who, among twentieth-century critics, writes better than Northrop Frye? Yet Frye is, by any account, a specialist. Force and euphony, it seems, can coexist with rhetorical refinement, as Frye and Trilling (here impressively cited, though, like Frye, not much admired at the present time) may be said to prove.

Indeed, Hartman comes quite close to saying that serious work on the arts, not least the literary arts, must be dull. Of course a great deal of it is; that is common ground. And he rightly says it has always been so, but I think not in quite the same way, the way in which critical prose seems to be constituted of offcuts picked up from the workshops of correct, determined, but, as it must appear to me, inadequate teachers. I would expect him to agree that since metalanguages came to seem more important or interesting than language, there are many more such teachers than there used to be.

As to "Resolution and Independence," what Hartman here says about it exhibits his long-established authority as a Wordsworthian. Yet I cannot agree that one must reject "pleasure / unpleasure" and install "unpower / power" as "the problematic subject." To say that the old man's powerlessness is the source of the poet's power is a way of justifying this substitution. Yet, as the opening lines of the poem insist, the power is expressed as pleasure (a Wordsworthian identification far from unique to this particular case). In the end, our views of this great poem are probably not as divergent as Hartman claims. But if we include imaginative readers in the equation, it might seem less plausible to claim that they share mainly in a process of "empowerment" than that they experience (in a manner appropriate to their humbler status) a movement of mind and emotion, "a peculiar, dangerous sort of inspiration" that has the complexities of "pleasure/unpleasure" offered by what we call great poetry. Here it seems perverse to discount pleasure in order to exalt power, though it could be said that power has a place in the argument as an inadequate analogical term for the exaltations of pleasure.

However, it is pleasant and not without importance that two imaginative readers (I make the claim for both of us) have remained certain over a lifetime that "Resolution and Independence" is wonderful without quite agreeing about why it is so. Others will offer different readings, no less imaginative. It must, in that sense, change. But why should it not also give pleasure?

Index